Stewart Home is the author of several books of fiction and cultural commentary, including *Defiant Pose*, *No Pity*, and *Neoist Manifestos/The Art Strike Papers*. His novels, *Slow Death* and *Come Before Christ and Murder Love* are also published by Serpent's Tail. He lives in London.

MIND

INVADERS

A reader in psychic warfare, cultural
sabotage and semiotic terrorism

Edited by Stewart Home

Library of Congress Catalog Card Number: 97–065848

A complete catalogue record for this book can
be obtained from the British Library on request

First published in 1997 by Serpent's Tail,
4 Blackstock Mews, London N4, and
180 Varick Street, 10th floor, New York, NY 10014
Web site: http://www.serpentstail.com

Set in 10pt Sabon by Intype London Ltd
Printed in Great Britain by Mackays of Chatham

CONTENTS

INTRODUCTION –
MONDO MYTHOPOESIS

It is incredibly difficult to summarise the bizarre developments that have taken place in what can be misrepresented as the 'underground' in recent years. The origins of the London Psychogeographical Association, the Association of Autonomous Astronauts and other even more bizarre groups are now obscure. The same can be said about the arguments taking place on private Internet servers such as the Invisible College. In line with the slogan 'anonymous elitism', participation in these forums is by invitation only. Those involved are forever covering their tracks and engineering faked feuds and public slanging matches. They use each other's names, as well as constructing collective identities that may be used by anyone, to foster anonymity.

If there is a precursor to all this activity, then it might be found in Neoism, an equally murky 'movement' said to have existed in Europe and North America during the eighties. Unfortunately, information is not only hard to come by, it is often unreliable. This point is illustrated by an anonymous Invisible College text headlined *Censorship is a More Popular Form of Subjectivity than Imagination*:

> The Neoist slogan 'It's always six o'clock,' for example, was coined by the Montreal Neoists Kiki Bonbon and Reinhardt U. Sevol, who used to beat up anyone who dared to ask them the time. tENTATIVELY, a cONVENIENCE and some East Coast Neoists campaigned for the 'friendly fascist' Vermin Supreme in Baltimore. With support from the graphic design

entrepreneur John Berndt, the Groupe Absence advocates radical free trade capitalism, while the godfather of Monty Cantsin, Dr. Al Ackerman, lifted the Neoist slogan 'Total Freedom' from his fellow science fiction writer and drinking buddy Lafayette Ron Hubbard. Of course, these anecdotes are not exactly 'authentic' . . .

All I can present here is a vortex of free associations, a chaotic overview of phenomena that are extremely difficult to categorise. How is one to describe hundreds of anonymous cultural 'terrorists' whose activities have coalesced into an autonomous literary genre? Imagine a 'heroic bloodshed' movie with rumours instead of bullets. Outside the UK, many people have been told that the person co-ordinating all this activity is Grant Mitchell, in 'reality' a character from the popular British soap opera *EastEnders*. Another tale slanders those engaged in 'avant-bardism' as recuperators who are infiltrating the revolutionary 'movement' to 'intoxicate' radicals with crazy theories. It goes without saying that claims of this type simply play into the hands of psychogeographers and autonomous astronauts. Indeed, it is widely believed that the individuals slandering the avant-bard are actually working hand in glove with them, in a bid to further publicise their activities!

Rebels and bohemians traverse cities scattering signs, staging enigmas, leaving coded messages, usurping the territorial claims of priests and kings by transforming the social perception of specific urban sites. Both the London Psychogeographical Association and the Manchester Area Psychogeographic use their newsletters to publicise regular gatherings that interested parties may attend. On these trips, anything or nothing at all may happen. These are possible appointments and sometimes only one intrepid psychogeographer attends. Other events are huge gatherings of urban tribes bent on emotionally remapping the cities in which they dwell. Psychogeographers pass each other like ships in the night, show up late or not at all.

A concrete example of all this activity is the Radio Blissett broadcasts from Bologna, which began in 1994 and ran for a year and a half. Radio Blissett was a late-night psychogeographical show in which every participant used the name Luther Blissett. Patrols were sent out into the city, where they were able to maintain contact with the studio via mobile phones. The patrols reported back on where they were and what they could see. They received suggestions about possible activities from listeners and proceeded accordingly. People called in requesting that the patrols do this or that, perhaps something as minor as buying a pizza and taking it to a specific address. The patrols drifted around the city, meeting up with listeners and incorporating the situations they encountered into the show.

In 1995, an autonomous Radio Blissett show began on a left-wing radio station in Rome. The Bolognese programme was broadcast midweek, the new one was aired on Saturday night when the streets were crowded, and there were more opportunities to create confusion. Actions included mass demonstrations with leaflets being handed out against proper nouns, there were also collective psychic attacks on bourgeois notions of identity. During a massive psychosexual be-in, thirty people decided they wanted to have full sex. They wrapped themselves in a huge cellophane sheet and began to caress each other. The petting got heavier, but before it could become a full-blown shag-in, it was broken up by the police. On 17 June 1995, a listener called the show and exhorted its audience to occupy a number 30 night bus. A merry band of psychogeographers boarded the bus with ghetto blasters blaring Radio Blissett. A police block stopped the bus in Piazza Ungheria. The illegal ravers moved onto a 29 bus, which in its turn was stopped by the cops in Guido d'Arezzo. The psychogeographers refused to surrender, and when the police assaulted them they fought back. A cop fired shots into the air. The riot and shoot-out were broadcast live via a mobile phone. Ten Luther Blissetts were arrested and charged with participation in a seditious rally.

These activities, like everything else, are a self-conscious construction. As such, the notions they utilise – including 'psychogeography', 'Luther Blissett' and 'fucking in the streets' – should not be viewed as arbitrary, but as self-contained signs. Everything done with these signs immediately effects what they are supposed to represent. 'Originally', both these modes of activity and the accompanying theorisation of them were simply fancies circulated in ephemeral forms, private systems of symbols shared among a number of international players. One popular psychogeographical game was to ornament these symbols by enshrining them within an allegorical form, creating fables that could only be deciphered by insiders. At some point, perhaps through forgetfulness, this insider knowledge was lost, and those playing this game had to continually reinvent it. Increasingly fantastic interpretations were made of these symbols, until avant-bardism became an 'art' of systematic contradiction, a self-refuting *perpetuum mobile*. In their sublime solemnity, such activities have had an extraordinary impact on those unenlightened by critical thoroughness.

Moving on, the Association of Autonomous Astronauts launched itself with picnics in different parts of Europe. In Windsor Great Park, just outside London, the consumption of food and drink was accompanied by a mass release of gas-filled balloons bearing the triple A logo. By way of contrast, events staged by the Workshop for a Non-linear Architecture are usually sparked by chance encounters and remain unplanned even as they unfold. Although these activities have been misrepresented as 'anarchist' or even 'avant-garde' by the press, it should go without saying that such strategic failures of the understanding fail to do justice to the omnidirectional attack of psychogeographical activity. Those involved in avant-bardism sometimes adopt positions that might be mistaken for 'occultism' or 'anarchism', but they do so solely as a means of dissolving these categories by pushing their internal contradictions to a 'logical' 'extreme'.

The avant-bard has no programme; it simply utilises practical methods to explore our 'world' of proliferating margins. Using maps of the Outer Hebrides, the Neoist Alliance spent one bracing winter day traversing Holbeach Marsh on the Wash. Here, the managed environment of fields and dikes ends at the sea walls. Nevertheless, even on the salt marshes uncovered by the tide, the influence of human domestication prevails – prior to reclamation, the sea lapped several miles further inland. The London Psychogeographical Association celebrated one solstice with a gathering at the Callanish standing stones on the Isle of Lewis. Despite the fact that nature has been rendered inorganic by the onslaughts of capitalism, with any meaningful distinction between the town and the countryside abolished, psychogeographers still see mysterious ley lines everywhere. Whether ley lines actually exist is irrelevant, as the widespread dissemination of astrological materials demonstrates, belief in mysterious 'phenomena' adversely effects the behaviour of millions. The satirical deconstruction of these beliefs is merely one achievement of the avant-bard.

Stewart Home

DECADENT ACTION MANIFESTO

Decadent Action

Decadent Action are the man and woman sitting next to you at the cocktail bar, they have money in their pockets and mischief on their minds.

Decadent Action are a High Street anarchist–guerrilla organisation whose main aim is to destroy the capitalist system by a leisurely campaign of good living and overspending. We plan to achieve our aims by making capitalism fall on its own sword. If you neglect and ignore capitalism it will not go away, but feed it to excess for long enough and it will eventually burst.

We use the simple economic principles of supply and demand with their intrinsic link to inflation to establish the correctness of our theories. The state must control these factors to run the economy efficiently; throw in the wild card of massive irrational overspending on seemingly random luxury goods and the government is unable to take control. This will lead to hyperinflation and large-scale social unrest, in turn leading to the collapse of the monetary system and disintegration of the state apparatus.

So how can you get involved in this conspiracy to overthrow the government without making too much effort or getting your hands dirty? Well, the answer is to spend, spend, spend! Get money, spend it; it's as simple as that. Below we set out ten pointers to help you to become truly decadent and to destroy the monetary system at your leisure.

1 Savings are for losers. When the monetary system

collapses your few pounds in the bank will become worthless. Get them out and blow the lot on a night out. We can recommend the Lanesborough Hotel on Hyde Park Corner in London, the Stannary in Tavistock (Devon) or just choose the best place nearest to you and hit the vintage champagne.

2 Shopping is fun, and you can never have enough designer labels, so buy that dress you've been lusting after. The words 'dry clean only' are what we look out for, and good quality clothing is available in all major towns and cities. Stylish clothes can get you into all the right (and wrong) places and can help you convince others of your wealth in order to pull a fast one.

3 Government sponsorship is always a nice way to fund a spending spree. This comes in many forms – dole money, business start-up grants, blackmail and bribery are all money for nothing. Try seeing how quickly you can blow your dole cheque in a cocktail bar.

4 Never ever eat chocolate of less than 60 per cent cocoa solids. Ackermans or Green & Blacks is what you should be eating.

5 Credit is the decadent's friend. It is inflationary, it is free money, it is fun to spend. Credit cards are best, yours or someone else's. Available now from high street banks, all you have to do is convince them that you can pay it back – a piece of piss. When the monetary system collapses your bill will simply disappear. Keep several credit cards with you at all times.

6 Shopping without money is an essential part of our plan. See it, like it, have it. Never take no for an answer.

7 Pass on the decadent message at all possible opportunities. We recommend writing, rubber stamping or scalding on bank notes with appropriate pro-consumer slogans such as 'SPEND, SPEND, SPEND' and 'SHOP NOW, RIOT LATER'.

8 Terrorism and violence against the state can be fun, but make sure you get the right tools for the job. Sawn-off shotguns are crude and could snag your clothes. In short, if you're going to shoot a cop – make sure you use a nice gun.

9 Guilt and the morals of the Christian Right have no place in our plans. Get yourself out and buy some smut, get down to your local perv shop and kit out your dungeon.

10 Sort out the right heroes and influences – take a tip from us and spend the day of the next general election in bed with a jug of your favourite cocktail and a Combustible Edison soundtrack, and read up on Baader, Meinhof, Chomsky, Susie Bright, Harry Roberts, Valerie Solanas, Viv Nicholson and troublemakers the world over. The odd few pence on a meagre minimum wage is not our concern when we want to bring the whole system crashing down.

These are just a few of the things that may help you in the war against the monetary system. Invitations to exclusive restaurants, gifts of fine wines and champagne are also encouraged.

First published in *The Idler*, January/February 1996.

MISSING PRESUMED DEAD

How Luther Blissett hoaxed the TV cops

Luther Blissett

Chi l'ha visto? is Italian for 'Has anybody seen them?' It is the name of a prime-time TV show whose presenters track down teenagers who have left home, wives who have deserted insolent husbands, patients who have escaped from the madhouse, and even draft dodgers. The editorial staff are an unofficial Vice Squad, while anchorwoman Giovanna Milella personifies everything that individuals who value freedom despise. Milella exudes middle-class values and exhorts the audience to co-operate in her weekly manhunts by calling in with information. The studio fills up with crying parents, angry wives or husbands, psychiatrists, the families and friends of the missing persons, and so on. In January 1995, Luther Blissett played a prank that placed the TV cops at *Chi l'ha visto?* in the pillory of media gossip.

Luther Blissett is a multiple name that can be used by anyone involved in cultural terrorism. Anyone who makes use of the name may invent a different story about the origin of the project. In Italy there is a rumour that a British body-artist called Harry Kipper borrowed the name from a Jamaican soccer player of the early eighties. At first Kipper used the name as a personal tag to sign his performances, then he decided to turn Blissett into an 'open character' whose reputation would be reinvented by anyone who cared to do so. Anyone can be Luther Blissett and inflate the reputation of this cultural terrorist simply by adopting the name and spreading new rumours.

Two Harry Kippers really existed, they were a UK-based body-art duo going by the name of the Kipper Kids, but they had nothing to do with the origin of this multiple name. Nevertheless, some of their performances became accessories to the Kipper legend, an Italian offshoot of the Luther Blissett Project. In November 1994, persons unknown decided to cement this originary myth by morphing male and female faces, thereby creating the only known portrait of the camera-shy Harry Kipper. Much later, this image became the androgynous icon through which Luther Blissett was manifested in the world of appearance. After we hit upon Harry Kipper as the imaginary founder of the Luther Blissett Project, the myths surrounding our activities developed along two distinct levels of simulation: those of the origin, which involved the ongoing creation of new details, and that of the multiple name itself. Even today, nobody knows what is true and what isn't.

In December 1994, Luther Blissett decided to stage the disappearance of the non-existent Harry Kipper, who we claimed had recently visited Italy. Rumours were spread until there was enough interest in the disappearance for us to successfully approach *Chi l'ha visto?* We laid false tracks so that many people suspected that the disappearance was in fact an allegory of the death of the artist being acted out by Harry Kipper. We made it plain that Kipper placed great stress upon the fact that the whole world is a manifold global performance in which everybody, whether conscious of it or not, plays a part in creating everything, and where no creation is wholly individual.

On the first level of simulation, Kipper had to free the Luther Blissett Project from identification with its actual founders and origins, to let it jettison ballast and take off. On the second level of simulation, the prank was an assault on *Chi l'ha visto?* and an opportunity to test the networking abilities of people using the multiple name. We fabricated a believable story, filled with half-truths, then gave it to a national news agency. On 3

January, ANSA spread the story from its offices in Udine, Friuli, in the northeast of Italy. The next day, not only was the story to be found in all the regional newspapers, but there was virtually no textual variation from our original fax to ANSA, who had used it wholesale. Here's an example from *Il messaggero veneto* of 1 April 1995:

AN ARTIST DISAPPEARS: S.O.S. FROM LONDON TO FRIULI

Last sighting in Bertiolo. He was touring Europe on a bike. Did he head towards Bosnia? Artists from Bologna and London are seeking information concerning the whereabouts of an Englishman called Harry Kipper, who disappeared in Friuli. He is 33 years old, has dark-red hair and magnetic blue eyes. Kipper, a.k.a. Luther Blissett, was a busker and a conjuror. There has been no news of him for ten weeks. The Bolognese artist Federico Guglielmi says Kipper was last seen leaving Bertiolo for Trieste. In the middle of October, Kipper telephoned his friend Stewart Home, a London-based novelist, and said he was in Bosnia. This was the last time anyone heard from him. Some Italian artists who knew Kipper have revealed that he was touring Europe on a mountain bike, linking different cities with an imaginary line that would eventually spell out the word 'ART'.

It was the Friulian artist Piermario Ciani who originally came up with the idea of linking cities to spell the word 'ART'. Last summer Kipper stayed in Ciani's house, since these two friends were keen to see the project bought to a successful conclusion. In early September, Kipper left for Trieste, but it seems he never arrived there. Kipper had begun his 'psychogeographical tourism' in 1991, when he traced the 'A' from Madrid to London and Rome. It took the next two summers to complete the 'R', through Brussels, Bonn, Zurich, Geneva and Ancona. In 1994, Kipper had begun the 'T'. From Trieste, he'd planned to visit Salzburg, Berlin and Warsaw, before returning to Amsterdam. Instead, he apparently made an inexplicable detour to Bosnia, where he disappeared.

Further details lifted from our fax were featured in other articles:

> Once Kipper arrived in Friuli, he decided to trace the word 'ART' through our region, starting from Pordenone. He reached Maniago, Sauris and Codroipo to trace the 'A', then Tolmezzo, Gemona, San Daniele and Mortegliano to trace the 'R' and finally Udine, Pontebba, Tarvisio and Treppo Carnico for the 'T'. Then he came back to Bertiolo.

The fax we'd sent to ANSA included Kipper's portrait, psycho-topographical maps of 'ART IN EUROPE' and 'ART IN FRIULI', plus the phone numbers of the Bolognese and Friulian 'artists' who'd put Kipper up. In reality, these were anarchists, transmaniacs, psychogeographers and so on. Piermario Ciani had first floated his psychogeographical projects some years previously, so this made our tale more convincing. On 6 January, the *Chi l'ha visto?* editorial staff phoned me in Bologna. They said they were fascinated by Kipper's story and wanted to cover his journey and disappearance from London to Bologna and Udine. I conferred with my comrades in London, Bologna and Friuli, before agreeing to take part in the show.

Four days later, a TV crew came to Bologna in order to reconstruct Kipper's journey and film his friends. They had some difficulty understanding what the fuck psychogeography was about! We told them that Kipper was in Bologna from 29 June to 8 July. He'd attended the founding of the Associazione Psicogeografica di Bologna, and suggested that all members adopt the multiple name Luther Blissett. Then he left for Ancona and the Adriatic Riviera. On 10 August he arrived in Udine, where he met Ciani at the Radio Onde Furlane studios. Ciani then suggested that Kipper trace the word 'ART' across the Friuli region. Three days later, Kipper went from Bertiolo to Pordenone to trace the 'A'. Two weeks passed before he was back in Bertiolo, claiming he had completed the word. However, rather than viewing this as a triumph, he seemed to be sad. At the beginning of September he headed for Trieste.

We heard nothing of Kipper's movements until a month after he phoned Stewart Home. It was then that Stewart called Ciani and the APB, and we began searching for our missing friend.

In January, the APB and Luther Blissett were still relatively unknown, so we were able to pass ourselves off as artists. A member of the TV crew called Fiore di Rienzo told us that the editorial staff assumed the disappearance was a piece of performance art being enacted by Kipper. Fucking idiots! The next day the TV cops went to Udine, where our comrades confirmed our account of Kipper's wanderings. There was even an article in the local rag, *Il gazzettino del Friuli* of 1 December 1994, to announce that *Chi l'ha visto?* was in town. In this piece the TV cops speculated that Kipper's disappearance might simply be a conceptual art work that the English artist was acting out.

Two days later the crew reached London and interviewed Stewart Home and Richard Essex of the London Psychogeographical Association. Stewart and Richard even showed them Kipper's old house, a half-demolished building in the East End. The show was about to be broadcast when a tip-off caused the TV cops to cancel it. Unfortunately, a freelance correspondent of *Chi l'ha visto?* living in Udine overheard a drunken conversation and concluded that not only was the disappearance a practical joke but so was Kipper's very existence. The editorial staff decided not to risk their reputation and replaced the announced programme at the last minute. However, this move was pointless because we'd already informed the press about the prank. The result was headlines such as *Cyber Prank on Chi l'ha visto?*, *They Made a Fool of Milella*, *Searching for Kipper who Doesn't Exist!* etc.

The papers reprinted parts of our explanatory statement. 'We wanted to do more than simply throw discredit on the show, we wanted to make them waste their time tracking a non-existent person, so that the real runaways could stay free', *Il resto del Carlino* of 20 January 1995 reported us as saying. '*Chi l'ha visto?* is a nazi-pop expression of the need to control', was the quote that *L'unità* of 21 January lifted from our press release. Our statement concluded with the observation that:

> This prank is the best proof yet of how effective multiple name techniques can be. The method allows many different revolutionary subjects to network without mistrust or paranoid suspicions, enabling them to effortlessly influence the collective imagination. This is much better than making useless complaints about the omnipotence of the spectacle. Become Luther Blissett!

Loosely translated from Italian; first issued as an instant Internet classic in 1995.

PISS MANIFESTO

Mandy B.

Hey! Stand and deliver . . . Girls. You've been brainwashed . . . it's the most practical thing to do. It makes sense. Get yourself on your feet and stand proud and piss with pride.

Why should us girls get germs off the toilet seat? No wonder we get spots on our arses as we're the ones who have to stick our bare flesh down that germ-stinkhole. ARRR!

In contemporary western society it is customary for the woman to sit or crouch, while the erect position is reserved for males. For the woman to urinate she is required to uncover herself and crouch. She has to hide, making the procedure of pissing shameful and inconvenient.

Her organ is secret, invisible and not to be grasped in the hand. In a sense she has no sex organ. For a boy, urinating is much more convenient. The penis can be manipulated, the stream can be directed at will and to a considerable distance.

GIRLS – THE FOLLOWING ARE INSTRUCTIONS FOR PISSING STANDING UP:

1 Before starting the piss
   (a) Position the feet either side of the toilet.
   (b) Make sure vagina is directly over the centre of the pan.
2 Warnings
   (a) You may have to pivot the pelvis according to direction and speed of flow. (This will prevent piss from going down the leg.)

3 Advantages of types of clothing worn
  (a) Dress and skirts – no problem if not too long and hippie-like.
  (b) Leggings – good for absorbing drips.
  (c) Jeans – as long as the waist isn't too tight (none of that seventies shit).

FACTS

According to a survey carried out by Cornell University in the USA, men spend an average of 45 seconds using a public toilet, while women take an average of 80 seconds. How the fuck this information was found I just don't know! You only need to sit down on the toilet if you are pregnant, in need of a poo, have blood to mop up or you're bloody tired. So the rest of you can stand – and it's so much quicker.

SO

Go with the directional flow girl. Pin those lips right back, whip them knickers down, don't worry 'bout any dribbles or slime trails down your legs. Pelvis thrust out, push strong and fast, don't worry if you spray at first, you'll soon get the hang of it. Have a quick grope while you're there and you'll be sorted.

First published in *Leisure* 4, Cardiff 1990, subsequently a bulletin board favourite.

OPEN UP THE NORTHWEST PASSAGE

London Psychogeographical Association

In 1566, Humfrey Gilbert initiated the campaign to open up the Northwest Passage. Four hundred years later the call was taken up by the Situationist International. George Gascoigne tells the reader in his introduction to Gilbert's *Discourse of a Discovery for a New Passage to Cataia* how his hero is akin to a bee in Queen Elizabeth's beehive who has waspishly gone astray, but yet at last returns to his former abiding. Gascoigne himself was a kinsman to Martin Frobisher, the Yorkshireman who first attempted the Northwest Passage.

It was during a visit to Humfrey Gilbert's home in Limehouse that he came upon Gilbert's text and arranged to have it published. He assures the reader that John Dee, founder of the British Empire, liked the text very much and that he commended the author in his preface to the English translation of Euclid. Gilbert cites both Plato and Ficino in support of his plan, mentions Roman coins found by the Spanish in American gold mines, and refers to the discovery of Europe by some Indians in 1160, when a storm forced them onto the coast of Germany. Gilbert was driven by the search for commodities, not Utopia.

Nearly 400 years later, the Situationist International assembled in Limehouse, searching for new passageways. This was a contentious conference, the last that Asger Jorn attended. It was only after Prem and the Nashists had left that the SI declared its resolve to follow a new direction:

At this moment of history when the task is posed, in the most unfavourable conditions, of reinventing culture and the revolutionary movement on an entirely new basis, the Situationist International can only be a Conspiracy of Equals, a general staff that does not want troops. It is a matter of finding, of opening up, the 'Northwest Passage' towards a new revolution that cannot tolerate masses of performers, a revolution that must surge over that central terrain which has until now been sheltered from revolutionary upheavals: the conquest of everyday life. We will only organise the detonation: the free explosion must escape us and any other control forever.

'The counter-Situationist campaign in various countries',
                          Internationale Situationiste 8, January 1963.

The LPA is holding a rally near the site of the alchemical laboratory of the Society of the New Art, an organisation set up by Gilbert, Lord Burghley and the Earl of Leicester (its exact location has yet to be determined). It was also in Limehouse that Gilbert wrote his proposal for an Elizabethan 'Achademy', a proposal that was eventually realised by his fellow Merchant Adventurer, Sir Thomas Gresham. Gilbert claimed to have constructed remarkable navigational machines, an area of work with which Gresham College was quick to concern itself. Outside the nearby library, there is a statue of Clement Attlee, the mass murderer who signed the authorisation for dropping the atom bomb on Hiroshima. The town hall across the road used to be a socialist reliquary, where Prince Kropotkin's table was kept. Alongside this were other relics of the communist saint, Sylvia Pankhurst. (She was beatified by the Ethiopian Orthodox Church, and given the title Debre). These were removed before work began on Canary Wharf. The rally will celebrate a whole year since the reemergence of the LPA at the Cave at Roisia's Cross.

First published in the *London Psychogeographical Association Newsletter* 3, Lughnassadh 1993.

NONE DARE CALL IT NIHILISM

Luther Blissett

Neoist aesthetics are characterised by the practice of plagiarism and the use of collective pseudonyms. Plagiarism is a means of attacking private property, while the adoption of the name Luther Blissett by all members of the Neoist Network is central to the movement's death struggle with capitalism.

Backtracking for a moment to the late sixteenth century, we find that playwrights such as Shakespeare and Marlowe often plagiarised plots and ideas from earlier writers. In this plagiaristic aspect of Elizabethan drama, we can discern a highly advanced form of proto-modernism.

Plagiarism was also particularly well used by Lautreamont/ Ducasse (1846–70). Similarly, the work of William S. Burroughs is heavily dependent on plagiarism in terms of both content and style. This is particularly noticeable in relation to the texts of Tzara and Artaud.

The great advantage of plagiarism as a literary method is that it removes the need for talent, or even much application. All you really have to do is select what to plagiarise. Enthusiastic beginners might like to start by plagiarising this essay. A hard-core nihilist might choose to plagiarise it verbatim, while those individuals who labour under the delusion that they are of a more artistic bent will probably want to change a word here and there – or even place the paragraphs in a different order!

It should not be forgotten that plagiarism is a highly creative exercise and that with every act of plagiarism a new meaning is brought to the plagiarised work. Unfortunately, this does not alter the fact that the capitalistic forces controlling Western culture have proscribed as illegal the plagiarising of modern texts. However, do not allow this to deter you from plagiarising modern work. A few sensible precautions will protect you from prosecution. The basic rule in avoiding copyright infringement is to take the idea and spirit of a text without actually plagiarising it word for word. One of the best examples of this is Orwell's *1984* – which is a straight rewrite of Zamyatin's *We*. Anyone with a serious interest in neo-plagiarism should spend some time comparing these two texts.

In the area of popular music, a good example of neo-plagiarism is the way in which the chord sequence was lifted from *Louie Louie* and married to the words of *Wild Thing*. This is plagiarism at its best, with no redeeming factors such as a clever change of context.

In short, plagiarism saves time and effort, improves results and shows considerable initiative on the part of the individual plagiarist. As a revolutionary tool, it is ideally suited to the demands of the late twentieth-century.

Compiled in the late eighties from texts in three year old issues of *Smile* magazine.

COUNTER-REVOLUTIONARY COMMUNISM

Monty Cantsin

1 The concept of 'Revolution' is inherently 'religious' and refers to an unrealisable abstraction. Those who act for the collective transformation of the world must reject the concept of revolution and all other concepts that locate change in an undefined and distant future. Until we have crushed the concept of revolution we will be slaves to history.

2 Dialectics are mystification. It is naive to assume that the interaction of ideas within social process will mechanically resolve social contradictions. The concept of historical inevitability is completely laughable. An understanding of 'history' shows the accumulation of 'contradiction', the identity of which is produced by the logical habits of the observer.

3 The emotional desires that are expressed as 'social theories' have never been rigorously 'scientific', and it is the worst mystification for revolutionaries to couch their agendas in a 'scientific' context. That a 'revolutionary' would want to is indicative of the general lack of critical engagement towards 'scientific thought' present in 'revolutionary' culture. Science is a fascist ideology which perpetuates itself through a technical elite that produces 'truth' in support of capitalism. It is based on a variety of false premises which remain relatively unchallenged. Most notable is science's reliance on 'cause and effect', a warped version of the capitalist ideology of 'individuality', positing 'individual causes' directly linked to individual 'effects' within a coherent universe. Though this concept is in practice highly elaborated, it has its roots in the fragmentary world view transmitted by capitalism. Communists should attempt to collectivise 'truth' and overthrow the scientific 'knowledge' that has brought destructive technology and industrial slavery.

4 'Revolutionaries' tend to engage the system only within their own minds, creating separate identities which 'self-manage' their alienation. To be a 'revolutionary' is to engage in a nostalgic fascist mythology, part of the entertaining stage-set of the 'Western world'. To achieve change it is imperative that all separate identities be destroyed along with the institutions and attitudes that support them.

5 'Community' is the abstraction by which ethnocentrism is reified on a local scale. The concept of the community, as an abstraction, further situates human life within the comprehensibility of a productive, receptive discourse outside its own control. To be part of a 'community' is to reinforce an identity as alienated as 'individual' identity. The resolution of the collectivisation of power stands outside the existence of banal and comprehensible cultures.

6 Massive change on a local or total level is possible and in process.

Mutating text that has been in circulation for several years; it lacks a fixed point of origin and has previously appeared in many different forms, often in several places at once.

JESUS WITH A HARD-ON

Luther Blissett

Male bonding plays a crucial role in German student fraternities. These societies are extremely hierarchical and within them even activities such as drinking are ritualised. Likewise, some fraternities still expect members to prove their masculinity in duels, and those who participate in these archaic rituals are actually proud of scars inflicted during the course of such *divertissements*. Naturally, women are excluded from the influential academic networks that grow out of the fraternities. The majority of fraternities trace their lineages back to the nineteenth century, and in the thirties and forties they actively supported the fascist state. Even those fraternities that didn't openly proclaim themselves in favour of Nazism made no attempt to resist their incorporation into the fascist system under which all organisations were controlled by state functionaries. With the unification of Germany, the fraternities are once again assuming reactionary *völkisch* positions.

In Tübingen, the student fraternities' annual May celebrations have encountered fierce opposition. Just before midnight on the last day of April, after an evening of ritual drinking, torch-lit processions make their way into the centre of town. Participants in this spectacle wear archaic costumes, including tiny caps and ribbons stretched across their chests, while coloured flags hang from their belts. They stop in Tübingen's ancient marketplace, where they sing songs. Fortunately, no one but the fraternity singers can hear this racket, since autonomes and liberals alike turn up to drown them out with everything from cat calls to renditions of *The International*.

At one time, there were violent brawls between the two sides. However, from the mid-eighties onwards, the fraternities have been protected from rotten eggs and other missiles by a massive police presence.

In 1995, after a decade long standoff, a group calling itself the Committee for Public Safety confronted the fraternity members with a new type of demonstration. A number of hoaxes added to the rumours and expectations surrounding the 1995 'celebrations'. First, a poster appeared in Tübingen University announcing a debate on the question 'Are German soldiers rapists and murderers?' The title of the discussion was a reference to the work of the satirical Weimar writer Kurt Tucholsky. The poster claimed the debate was organised by the highly respectable Association of German Students, and that the speakers would include Walter Jens, a famous liberal academic, who'd be opposed by a conservative professor of law. Needless to say, the discussion never took place. Second, the local newspaper printed a number of fake letters whose authors claimed they were fraternity members. One particularly ridiculous missive even featured a complaint about the ban on the wearing of fraternity colours, which the Allies placed in 1945, still being in force.

On the night of the ritual, the fraternity members suffered further ridicule. Although the torch-lit processions went off without a hitch, having made their way to the marketplace, disaster struck when the reactionary students began to sing. First, massively enlarged slides were projected onto the front wall of the church that dominates the square. The slides included photographs of Hanns-Martin Schleyer, a business leader killed by the Red Army Faction, and various Nazi war criminals. These were followed by a grinning Nuremberg hangman offering his noose to Nazis who'd been condemned to death. By this time, the audience gathered in the square had lost interest in the torch-carrying reactionaries. People began to laugh. After the slide-show, the fraternity boys made another attempt at singing their songs. Despite cop protection, the student reactionaries were drowned out by *Conquest of Para-*

dise, thanks to the powerful public address system that autonomes had installed in a flat in the square. The Vangelis tune is particularly well known in Germany, since it is played whenever the sporting champion Henry Maske enters a boxing ring.

Next, twelve naked men emerged from a marketplace flat rented with the specific intention of providing a means of realising this intervention, and danced across the square, which the cops wrongly assumed had been completely sealed off. The nude autonomes stood on the stairs of the church, where some of them swung their arms in the air, while others unfolded banners emblazoned with the message 'Jesus loves us all'. With banners unfurled, the autonomes advanced towards the fraternity-men, then towards the crowd. The police attempted to keep them away from the singers – but nothing could stop the autonomes. The student reactionaries were baffled. They'd stopped singing and some were so angry they wanted a fight. The police held them back. Others laughed, humming along to Vangelis.

The twelve autonomes handed Christian leaflets to the cops, the fraternity members and the crowd that had gathered to watch the spectacle, then slowly retreated across the square. The nude autonomes climbed over crowd-control barriers. Cops whose orders were to prevent protesters from storming the marketplace had no idea what to do about naked demonstrators making their way out of the 'sealed' square. The crowd received the autonomes enthusiastically, lifting them up onto a fountain, where they sang a modern Christian song, while the slide-show kicked off again. The fraternity members abandoned their celebrations, so the cops removed the crowd-control barriers. Protesters and spectators made their way into the square. From a side street, the muffled sound of thumping techno grew louder. A van rolled through the pedestrian precinct announcing an autonome rave in a nearby building.

The local paper reported the Committee of Public Safety intervention with a photograph of the twelve naked men, while a whole page was devoted to the demonstration in the national press. Obviously, this didn't cause the fraternities to close down, and their offensive posturing still needs to be challenged. Nevertheless, it showed that the political happening could unite the left and the underground in their opposition to the ritual domination of a specific public space by *völkisch* reactionaries.

Loosely translated and savagely abridged from the German. The full German text appears in *Handbuch der Kommunikationsguerilla* by Luther Blissett, Karen Eliot and autonome a.f.r.i.k.a.-gruppe (Edition Nautilus, Hamburg, 1997).

FREEDOM THROUGH MOVEMENT

Towards a molecular theatre

Ross Birrell

I

Artaud's theatre of cruelty has been betrayed by those who have refused the call to a political theatre. Artaud was a true rebel and as such he was opposed to the closed cyclical nature of permanent revolutions which necessarily sow the seeds of oppression in their conception; rather Artaud's was the rhizomorphic open structure of the temporary insurrection. Insurrections, invisible or otherwise, are the zones of potential for human freedom. The order of chaos.

Theatre is a transitory autonomous zone (this should not be confused with the '*T.A.Z.*' described by the reactionary traditionalist 'Hakim Bey'/Peter Lamborn Wilson in his book of the same name) and as such it is truly molecular, rhizomorphic, ever in non-dialectic opposition to molar structures of state, family, police, school, even theatre itself.

This is what we mean when we say 'theatre does not exist', as true theatre cannot present itself, it escapes arrival, it is forever on the move, nomadic; that is to say it is everywhere and nowhere, it does not exist, not yet anyway. It is a 'becoming' not a 'happening'.

Artaud's call for 'no more masterpieces' is realised in his image of the actor. The performer/actor is the sacrifice burned at the stake of bourgeois morality and values 'signalling through the flames' to no new horizon. This is the martyrdom of the trickster/revolutionary. Creation at the moment of death, language without words, deadly hieroglyphics, where the rest is done by screams.

Hence our mistrust of words in this manifesto in our recognition of their futility in communicating the full potential of the molecular theatre, which we believe can only be achieved in performance.

II

Performances will be free and only take place in public spaces. Performances will not be given to satisfy a desire constructed through boredom as in the traditional 'gift' of culture from the bourgeoisie to the proletariat (who had paid for it anyway); rather they will be taken, i.e. a seizure of the means of theatrical production where the actor and that sacred cow of the holy theatre, the director, will be slaughtered and delivered to the tramp as his midnight feast, to be replaced by anyone committed to the goals of the molecular theatre: freedom, chaos and fun!

This is what we mean by political theatre, the advocation of fun, recognising the potential of desire as a political force, as a line of flight from oppression, but picking up a weapon as we flee, and that weapon is movement.

The molecular theatre is a nomad, deterritorialising theatre, resisting definition, a new Living Theatre, only this time we know where the real targets are and how to hit back!

III

It must never be forgotten that some of the targets of the molecular theatre lie within ourselves and it is the fascism within that must be exposed in open combat.

We must destroy everything that prevents the reclamation of the body as an autonomous site in the struggle of the rebel against authority and oppression, which is the foundation of a truly spontaneous culture.

Spontaneous culture can only ever be temporary in nature;

that is why its true expression comes in the form of performances staged upon the theatre of the world . . .

DADAnarchist Manifesto I. First published by Semtex(t): Poverty Press, Glasgow, 1994.

TEN-POINT GUIDE TO BEING A CULT ARTIST

Luther Blissett

Contemporary art knows it's the new rock and roll. Successful young British artists like Damien Hirst crop up everywhere – from society gossip columns to the features pages of *Hello!* magazine. So if you fancy attending upmarket social gatherings and being driven around in a limo, then why not try your hand at cultural terrorism? Becoming a *nouveau* is easy. It certainly doesn't require any talent. Here's how to do it.

1 **RECOGNITION:** It's your image that sells the product. This is the ultimate form of branding. Gilbert and George are famous as the artists who wear business suits. Create a visual look and stick with it.

2 **PLAGIARISM:** Originality is for losers. Don't waste time on researching and developing new ideas – let others do this for you. Famous artists are inspired by their less successful peers, the ones who starve in garrets. Necessity might be the mother of invention, but there's no point in going hungry when you could be funding meals in expensive restaurants through acts of cultural theft. Cindy Sherman is famous for making photographic versions of Old Masters.

3 **NUDITY:** Former stockbroker turned art superstar Jeff Koons married the Italian porn queen Cicciolina and then used her as a model in his work. Everyone is interested in sex, which is why tits and bums are the favourite subject matter of great artists. So don't waste

your time with 'deep' subjects. Everything seedy is grist to the cult artist's mill. Since they've no experience of street life, rich art patrons are always attracted to decadent, debasing and degenerate subject matter. Select topics that are considered taboo.

4 EGOISM: If you don't believe in yourself, then nobody else will. You must make extravagant claims for your work. Sow confusion, so that even professional critics doubt their ability to correctly judge the value of the things that you do. Modern art is like the Emperor who had no clothes, as long as its unfounded claims about giving access to a higher realm of experience remain unchallenged, the rich and gullible will continue to invest money in stuffed sharks and houses filled with concrete. The highly successful Danish painter Asger Jorn once claimed that 'artistic research is identical to human science, which for us means concerned science, not purely historical science'.

5 PUBLICITY: Most successful artists begin their careers by praising their own work under a variety of pen names. While homages of this type rarely make it into the national press, the letters pages of obscure art journals are filled with them. As you become increasingly successful, your sheer financial clout will force critics to pay attention to your work. The glossy catalogue accompanying the recent exhibition *Chaos II* by Scandinavian artist Jens Jorgen Thorsen was filled with over-the-top praise from art critics. In fact, Thorsen was responsible for all the writing in the catalogue, which included an essay entitled *Jens Jorgen Thorsen's Paintings Defy the Laws of Gravity.*

6 ADDICTION: Heroin, crack and other hard drugs do nothing to aid the creative process, but the general public likes to believe that the 'genius' has no control over his or her creative outpourings. Therefore, it is necessary to cultivate the image of addiction without actually becoming an addict. All sorts of ruses can be used, from having needle marks tattooed up your arms to pouring gallons of whisky down the sink and then littering your studio with the empty bottles.

7 INCITE THE YOUNG AGAINST THE OLD: Art lovers are mainly old and rich; if you bad-mouth them in public, they will shower you with money and gifts. Your abusive words feed their delusion that it's possible to buy into the culture of the young and hip. However, do make sure that you know how to hold a knife and fork correctly. You must be on your best behaviour when spending the weekend at the family seat of important patrons. The works of the futurist group are collected by museums precisely because F.T. Marinetti, the leader of the movement, wrote that futurism 'will destroy the museums, libraries, academies of every kind'.

8 DON'T GET YOUR HANDS DIRTY: Andy Warhol, the most successful artist of the post-war period, had a huge entourage of assistants to help ease the tedium of the creative process. So pay someone else to make your work. A successful artist is a middle-class professional, not an artisan. The cult artist is only interested in the bottom line.

9 MARRY MONEY: There are two kinds of capital: financial and cultural. The cult artist wants both. The successful artist exploits the old maxim that fools and their money are easily parted. Selling a work of art is a one-off transaction. If someone wealthy is rash enough to marry you, then you can make them pay through the nose for their folly. The English painter Ralph Rumney was big news in the late fifties. After he married into the art-loving and super-rich Guggenheim family, his painting became something of a hobby.

10 DEATH: Great artists are popularly perceived as being immortal. Nevertheless, if the value of your work suddenly erodes, then death is often the smartest career move. Faking your own suicide and then disappearing is relatively painless; doing it for real requires the kind of commitment that exposes your assimilation into the *haute-bourgeoisie* as having been, at best, partial. It is the cult artist's output, and not the artist, that is supposed to be vulgar. New York artist Jean-Michel Basquiat was a hot property in the mid-eighties; when it all went wrong he topped himself and a retrospective show of his paintings is currently on at the prestigious Serpentine Gallery in Kensington Gore.

First published in the *Big Issue*, 25 March 1996.

NAZI OCCULTISTS SEIZE OMPHALOS

London Psychogeographical Association

The election of Derek Beackon as a Councillor on the Isle of Dogs caused shocked outrage across the Establishment. Beackon is a dedicated Nazi occultist. He graduated to the British Nationalist Party after serving his apprenticeship in the British Movement. Beackon is an adept of Enochian magic. Devised in the sixteenth century by John Dee, it was this magical system that laid the basis for the conjuring up of the British Empire. Like every other form of nationalism, British nationalism is a psychic elemental which drains energy from living people in order to maintain itself as a sickly caricature of life.

From his home at Mallon House, Carr Street, Limehouse, Beackon was able to tap into the powerful ley line running through his front room. This ley line is readily visible from the Observatory at Greenwich. It goes through the macabre Queen Anne House, and guided by the symmetry of the Naval College it crosses the Isle of Dogs, clipping the corner of Canary Wharf complex before exactly passing through the tower of St Anne's Limehouse. Then it passes through Beackon's lair before going on to Queen Mary and Westerfield College.

This ley line has been in the hands of the Establishment for years. They used the Greenwich section for astrological purposes. Time and space are measured from here. The British Establishment have now gained universal recognition for their hermetic system. Meanwhile, the other section at QMWC has been the centre of sub-atomic research. Thus Greenwich accounts for the macrocosm, while the alchemical processes north of the river account for the microcosm.

Many people believe that Greenwich is in fact the omphalos – or spiritual centre – of the British Empire. However, those with a deeper understanding of feng shui, the ancient Chinese art of land divination, will recognise that the actual omphalos must be on the Isle of Dogs, protected by water on all sides. Those who visit the Mudchute – a piece of park mysteriously built as an exact replica of an ancient hill-fort – will find a special staircase leading to a cobbled circle. This is the omphalos, the spiritual centre, where the magus John Dee conjured up the British Empire in the presence of Christopher Marlowe, four hundred years ago this year. However, using the ley line for such evil purposes necessitated the sacrifice of a human life. A psychic attack on Christopher Marlowe and his friends in a Deptford pub led to a brawl in which the famous playwright died.

In more recent years, the Canary Wharf tower was built very carefully. It is in fact a column supporting a pyramid at the top. This pyramid serves to represent the much larger pyramid that would be formed if the lines at each corner were stretched down to ground level. This greater 'virtual' pyramid lies with its southwest corner upon the ley line. The use of such street names as Cabot, Chancellor and Churchill clearly shows the intention to make Canary Wharf a powerful totem to resist the revival of German imperialism. Wren's name is used in deference to the architect who organised the building of the Naval College, and supervised the erection of St Anne's tower as a U-Wave conductor. The building of Canary Wharf involved several human sacrifices, passed off as 'accidents'.

However, the British establishment did not think that the pro-German British Nationalist Party would challenge them on this power line. But the BNP knew what price they would have to pay. Having conducted his obscene rituals to gain electoral success, Beackon fled his home, fearing the negative karma that would result. The BNP cynically pretended that he was in hiding from some unspecified anti-racists. Richard Edmonds, another cowardly BNP occultist, was so worried he arranged for some BNP moles in the police to keep him locked up in a cell, out of harm's way. However, the karmic law is remorseless. The power of the ley line having been used, a human life had to be sacrificed.

As the principal culprits had protected themselves from psychic attack, another top Nazi occultist would be the victim. It was Ian Stuart, lead singer of the cult band Skrewdriver. The official story is that the car he was travelling in crashed, and that the two passengers in the back escaped before the vehicle became a ball of fire. However, the truth is that the driver succumbed to demonic possession before spontaneously bursting into flames. The BNP may feel safe now that their demonic master has sated its hunger. But the BNP are mere amateurs at occultism when compared to the top experts who run the British Establishment. The more they proceed with their occult nightmare of ritualistic sadism, the more they become victims of Masonic mind control.

The British Establishment is now using them to conduct an experiment on the people of the Isle of Dogs. Using the Island as crucible of social engineering, they want to test what role race riots can play in propping up their decadent Masonic system. If the experiment goes wrong, the island can be sealed off and the inhabitants isolated. If it succeeds, the state will have a new weapon in its arsenal of terror.

Already, the *East London Advertiser* is running a competition where readers are invited to ring different phone lines to say whether they think it was right that the BNP were elected. This is simply another wing of the establishment experimenting with the Nazi impetus. We cannot expect the press to expose the evil of which they are in fact a part, albeit in a different department. The same goes for the rest of the establishment, whether the police, the church or the political apparatus. We can only move forward by having nothing to do with any of these evil organisations.

First issued as an undated leaflet.

LADDISM AND LABYRINTH

BD

A recent report from the government's Office of Population Censuses and Surveys confirms Manchester as having the highest death rate for men between 1989 and 1993. Manchester, therefore, that cultural centre of laddishness, so effortlessly and eloquently expressed in the conurbation's football clubs and pop groups, is strangely enough also a killer of lads. Is there something self-destructive about the multiple, industrialised male – explaining, perhaps, how the northwest region produced so many sacrificial 'lads regiments', slaughtered in Flanders during the First World War?

Militarism and the massed, armed male have had an influence on Manchester's growth from the time of the Romans onwards. The Roman fort and town of Mancunium, built at Castlefield, overlooked the road linking the legionary bases of Chester and York, at the point where it crossed the Irwell. A Roman temple unearthed in Hulme in 1821 was dedicated to Mithras, a sun deity with Persian origins, who enjoyed a cult following in the army. Worship of Mithras during the latter stages of the Roman Empire rivalled that other popular cult, Christianity, and shared similarities with it, including emphasis on the immortality of the soul. Typically, the Hulme temple was built to the southwest of the fort, and would probably also have faced west. Many temples to Mithras were also partially subterranean and utilised a single window to let a beam of light into the overall gloom to illuminate the altar. Mithras was often shown killing a bull – a symbol of seasonal, or sun-dominated, death, and of rebirth. He would often be accompanied in his British temples by accessory characters. One of the carvings found in Hulme depicted the Romano-British deity Cautopates, who was depicted burying a torch into the ground.

This subterranean world of darkness, representing death, is also remembered now in the form of the labyrinth or maze pattern, described in the Theseus/Minotaur legend, but also repeated endlessly in designs found in Britain and Europe on church floors and cut into turf. The labyrinth of tunnels dug underneath London in the nineteenth century, and used and extended subsequently for military and security purposes, has been well documented.

Manchester has never had a public underground railway service, but it does have a thriving anecdotal network of tunnels, workings and cities beneath the streets. Rumour has it that the most recent project to get an equivalent to the Tube operating during the late 1970s (the so-called Picc–Vic line) was prevented by the existence of a system of bunkers and rail lines creating a Regional Seat of Government (RSG) beneath Piccadilly Station – part of the network that would have come into action in the event of nuclear war during the sixties. More rumours have been circulating recently about the discovery of part of this 'secret city' being discovered in 1995 by Nynex cable TV workers, who were promptly ordered to fill the cavity they had unearthed with several tons of concrete. It is tempting to speculate on the geographical alignment along which Piccadilly Station, Manchester Town Hall and Crown Square all lie: a GPO cable and/or rail link may conceivably have been laid during the 1960s as a feature of the RSG.

Dozens of other stories exist concerning tunnels under Manchester and Salford, many centring on the Cathedral and Corn Exchange, in the heart of the Saxon and early medieval town of Manchester. Here, notably, is where John Dee, Elizabethan mathematician, geographer, astrologer and alchemist, lived when he was Warden of the Collegiate Church (before it became a cathedral). Remains of Dee's house are supposed to be preserved under the Corn Exchange, which was built over earlier street levels. Oddly enough, the original Victorian Corn Exchange, opened in 1837, was a copy of a Roman temple to Ceres on the River Ilyssus. Ceres, the Roman equivalent of the Greek Demeter, was goddess of crops and vegetation. For six months of every year she withdrew her influence on the world, in mourning for her daughter Persephone, who had been lured into the underworld by Pluto (equivalent of the Greek Hades).

It follows quite naturally that the Corn Exchange should now be a focal point for all manner of obscurantist, occultist concerns. Beliefs vary from stories about Dee performing rituals in the cellars under the Church to the Corn Exchange being the focal point for a series of powerful ley lines. The occult and the political/military complex, guarded by their surface elites, shrouded in secrecy, express their influence upon the modern city via symbols that literally undermine the everyday world of streets given over to increasingly simulationist consumerism.

And now, the 1996 Situationist conference in Manchester reminds us 'games are forbidden in the labyrinth', a theme that has constantly haunted Manchester's geographic and geomantic existence. Funny to think how the Hacienda, which plays host to conference, and which owes its moniker to the Situationist project, now forms one of several focal points for the posturing and prevarications of young male gang followers most weekend evenings. Ah, the lure of the basement . . .

We want to lift the lid on the subterranean power-circuit. Consequently, we have decided to gather on the 400th anniversary of Dr Dee's arrival in Manchester, at a point near his probable home, with a view to the levitation of the Corn Exchange. Anyone sympathetic, please meet us outside the aforementioned building, on the corner of Hanging Ditch and Cathedral Street, on Saturday 10 February, at 11.00 a.m.

First published in *Manchester Area Psychogeographic* 2, January 1996.

SMASH THE OCCULT ESTABLISHMENT

May 10th, National Maritime Museum, Greenwich

London Psychogeographical Association

The Queen and Baron Greenwich (a.k.a. Prince Philip) will be making a ritual visit to a site of key Masonic importance – the Queen Anne House, Greenwich. The Royal Greenwich Observatory have published their expectation for an annular eclipse on this day commencing at 3.12 p.m. (BST), reaching its greatest point at 6.19 p.m. (twelve minutes after the New Moon) The event will be finished by 9.10 p.m.

The ostensible reason for the visit is to celebrate the 300th anniversary of the founding of Greenwich Hospital. The Queen will attend a parade by pupils of the Royal Hospital School. However, the actual anniversary of the charter founding the Royal Hospital of Greenwich was 25 October 1694. So this choice of date implies precise astrological knowledge. Queen Mary, the founder of the hospital, almost immediately had an argument with top Freemason Sir Christopher Wren, the Surveyor-General who offered his services free. Wren wanted to pull down Inigo Jones's Queen Anne House and replace it with a domed chapel. The Queen said that Jones's building must stay, and must still have a view of the river – and so it was to be.

The Royal Hospital of Greenwich provided relief and support for seamen from the Royal Navy. In 1798 a bequest by Samuel Travers established the Naval Knights of Windsor; these were in addition to the eighteen poor Knights of Windsor, and they used to live on the terrace facing the gardens of the Dean and Chapter of Windsor. This is, of course, the HQ of the top occult order in Britain, the Order of the Garter. This double coven was founded by Edward III, with himself leading one group of thirteen, the other led by the Black Prince. These covens were originally battle-hardened fighting formations. The Bishop of Winchester *ex officio* had the role of Prelate, while the Dean resided at Windsor and kept the registrar. Sir Christopher Wren's father held this position, and Wren grew up in the environs of Windsor castle from his second to his ninth year. The Naval Knights of Windsor were dissolved in 1892, their funds now being managed by the Greenwich Hospital Estate.

Since 1873 the buildings towards the river have constituted the Royal Naval College. Vice Admiral Sir Astley Cooper Key, the first president, was a Fellow of the Royal Society, as was Dr Archer Hirst, the first Director of Studies. Many royal figures have attended the College, and Yeltsin was entertained in the Painted Hall – the officers mess.

We have already described how the Queen Anne House is aligned with a major ley line going through Beackon's flat. Its architect, Inigo Jones, has been singled out by Frances Yates as one of the key figures in the development of speculative Freemasonry in the first part of the seventeenth century. She has described how he may well have visited the magico-scientific gardens of Heidelberg when Queen Anne's daughter married the Elector of the Palatinate. In *The Rosicrucian Enlightenment,* she claims this marriage was of great importance in the generation of the Rosicrucians. Many of the goals of the Rosicrucians came to be realised when the Royal Society was set up after one of Wren's lectures in his capacity as a Gresham Professor of Astronomy. There is evidence that Wren was head Freemason at the time.

Although the occult significance of the site predates Inigo Jones (it has been claimed that there was a Temple to Apollo upon the site, and it certainly appears to be the spot where Sir Walter Raleigh threw down his cloak over a puddle for Queen Elizabeth I), the Queen's visit confirms the place's ritual significance. While we don't have space here to cover all the elements of Masonic furniture to be found in the vicinity, enough has been said to alert people to the occult role of the monarchy and encourage a collective response to it. Some people say they are not monarchists, but that republics are just as bad. That is like someone suffering from a disease refusing a cure because they might catch something else.

When we advocate the abolition of the monarchy, we are not advocating contracting the disease of republicanism; we are suggesting a move towards a healthy society free of all oppression and exploitation, a classless society.

First published in the *London Psychogeographical Association Newsletter* 6, Beltane 1994.

VIVA NEOISM

Luther Blissett

Neoism is a cultural movement influenced by Futurism, Dada, Fluxus and Punk, which emerged from the Mail Art Network in the late seventies.

Neoism is a methodology for manufacturing art history. The idea is to generate interest in the work and personalities of the various individuals who are said to constitute the movement. Neoists want to escape from 'the prison of art' and 'change the world'. With this end in mind, they present capitalist society with an angst-ridden image of itself.

Anyone can become a Neoist simply by declaring themselves to be a part of the movement and adopting the name Luther Blissett. However, Neoists don't restrict themselves to using the name Luther Blissett, they use the name Smile too. Neoists call their pop groups Smile, their performance groups Smile – even their magazines are called *Smile*.

This is a genuine existential experiment, it is an exercise in practical philosophy. Neoists wish to determine what happens when they cease to differentiate between assorted artefacts and individuals.

However, while Neoists place their faith in practical philosophy, they DO NOT endorse the study of logic as pursued in the universities and other authoritarian institutes. Neoist philosophy is to be tested on the streets, in pubs and night clubs; it involves the creation of a communist culture – not theoretical abstractions.

Capitalism masters the material world by naming and describing those objects it wishes to manipulate. By rendering names meaningless, Neoists destroy the central control mechanism of bourgeois logic. Without these classifications, Power cannot differentiate, divide and isolate the revolutionary masses.

Because they are sick of the fragmentary world in which they live, the Neoists have agreed to adopt a common name. Every action carried out under the banner of Luther Blissett is a gesture of defiance against the Order of Power – and a demonstration that the Neoists are ungovernable. Luther Blissett is a true individual in a world where real individuality is a crime!

Ultimately, Neoist philosophy is a revolutionary project which is undertaken with a view to improving the lot of mankind. Neoism supersedes all previous philosophies because it consciously founds itself on rhetoric rather than factual observation.

Neoists believe in the value of fraud as a revolutionary weapon. They practise an impure science and regularly fake their results. Using this methodology, Neoism has effortlessly refuted the dominant illusions connected to the mental set 'individuality' and now claims its right to slaughter all those who refuse to realise their true humanity. The success of Neoism is historically inevitable. LONG LIVE LIFE!

Compiled in the late eighties from texts in five-year-old issues of *Smile* magazine.

THE LUTHER BLISSETT MANIFESTO

Luther Blissett

Luther Blissett is the funny man in a farce staged on the theatre of the world. Luther broadens traditional notions of social struggle to encompass everything that is positive in contemporary urban folk culture. The manipulation and overthrow of the language of myths is Luther's starting point. He ransacks the archetypes of popular culture, as well as those thrown up by techno-Pagan religious revivalists. Luther Blissett is not the product of a pre-democratic and pre-individual view of the world that lays claim to a despotic social unity. Avant-bardism is a lucid shamanism that places itself *beyond* democracy and individuality.

As a Druid, Luther Blissett supports free chaotic empathy between all creatures. Luther, herself, is a charming transsexual foot fetishist – Paco Ignacio Taibo meets Paracelsus at an Illegal Rave. Luther Blissett challenges, tricks and cajoles wo/mankind to do far more than simply face the Abyss. Luther's jokes impel people to stare into the black depths of the pit; her jests wake sleepwalkers. Contemporary social relations are simply a highly contagious neuro-epidemic. Luther *plays into* this Catastrophe by tying her symbolic capital to it, and by these desperate means keeps the Northwest Passage open. The Multiple Name becomes a borderline experience, a live broadcast from the last promontory of the centuries. By exploring every conceivable avenue down which it is possible to escape the shackles of a conventional identity, Luther infuses the world with a fresh vitality.

It is a banality to state that the nihilistic tyranny of the spectacle is best fought by talking outrageously and telling tall stories. In other words, by raising a whirl of fibs and lies *until a communication short-circuit dissipates this virtual world and the real one appears again*. In fact, radical criticism of the world, indeed even the right to criticise it, was the overarching achievement of 'plagiarist' pirates of past centuries, of rascals, buffoons and court jesters. Feudal social conflicts were similar to those of the present day. The language of Kings and Popes – of the Law, the State and Social Rank – was challenged, perverted and undermined through plagiarism and parody. Resistance through lies kept language fluid and frustrated all attempts at systematic codification. Tramps, tumblers and troubadours avoided sanctioned forms such as courtly poetry and chivalrous romance, favouring instead despised genres such as satire, coarse songs and blasphemous prayers.

It was down-at-heel bards and minstrels whose linguistic cross-fertilisations bloomed, while the patronage of the mighty caused culture to shrivel on its stem. Thanks to the vast ranks of Druid dervishes, the speech of various classes, cultures, districts and professions modified and reinvigorated one another. The sixteenth-century novel *Gargantua et Pantagruel* by François Rabelais owes its radical outlook and subversive charge to the influence of merry bardic pranksters. By destroying every ideological partition between ideals and things, Rabelais clearly anticipated and influenced the theorising of Bakhtin. It has, of course, always been necessary to ignore tradition and let discourse fornicate and multiply, so that the order of things may be overthrown and culture created anew. It ought to go without saying that despite the constant intervention of an authoritarian ruling class, which wants to freeze life into a glacial hierarchy, diverse phenomena cannot be prevented from blending and clashing in all their concreteness and variety.

Rabelais, Villon and their anonymous predecessors didn't waste their breath attempting to articulate Truth in a world filled with lies. Instead, bards and minstrels 'circumvented' official truth and turned it inside out by pushing its logic to a paradoxical extreme. Even today, waging war against the language of the powers that be remains an integral part of the class struggle. The prank is the weapon by which we create new links between things and destroy all hierarchies. Just as Rabelais insisted the Middle Ages were over and that new social relations were liquidating the feudal world, so our task is to denounce wage labour as an obsolete social form that will disappear in the wake of our cyber-revolution. However, rather than simply waiting for cathartic explosions to destroy the capitalist system, we must speed up this process with strategically planned pranks.

The ruling class isn't going to grant us free access to the data banks their information revolution revolves around. We must challenge the very ways in which knowledge is ordered and thus end bourgeois rule. Once again, we must raise the spectre of chaos. Rumours and noise must be spread through every conceivable channel of communication, until it is generally recognised that a single one of our jests or lies carries more relevant information than all the police dossiers in the world. The 'morals' of those who ride the waves of the digital ocean are necessarily provisional. Until recently, those at the forefront of this tendency in Italy were known as transmaniacs. From the furthest depths of the Net plumbed by these mind invaders, the old prank of a *multiple identity* has boiled up again and will soon overflow the entire globe. The technique was overhauled by the Neoists in the mid-eighties, when Karen Eliot was an important multiple name; now it has been souped up by former Transmaniacs.

The Luther Blissett Project was launched in Summer 1994 by an international gang of revolutionaries, mail artists, poets, performers, underground 'zines, cybernauts and squatters. A multiple name, if used outside small circles of radicals, is a practical solution to problems such as the relationship between the individual and the community, or the quest for identity. All the debates over Nomadology and endless idle chatter about the creation of 'situations' are superseded by this concept. Luther Blissett is a *-dividual*, because she has many personalities and numerous reputations. Luther Blissett is also a *con-dividual*, because many people share the name. Luther Blissett is a multitude as well as a decentred subject. Luther Blissett is what Marx called Gemeinwesen, the common essence of wo/mankind, awareness of the global community. Luther Blissett is not an (anti)artist like Karen Eliot. She is a cultural terrorist who nevertheless supports the religious programme of the Neoist Alliance. Sabotages, hoaxes, urban legends, performances, magazines, bulletin boards and TV or radio broadcasts are spreading the name all over the world. This prank is constantly hitting new heights. Anyone can be Luther Blissett simply by adopting the name. Plug into the General Intellect, become Luther Blissett before Luther Blissett comes gunning for you.

Originally composed in Italian and placed on the Net in May 1995, this English language version bears little resemblance to the first provisional translation, which was accompanied by a request that it should be rewritten by everyone who found themselves in agreement with its theses.

WHO RULES BRITAIN?

London Psychogeographical Association

The survival of a pampered elite living in the lap of luxury while more and more homeless people are thrown on the streets, while the poorest 15 per cent of the population have their standard of living slashed yet again – the survival of this gang of 'beautiful people' rests on their ability to rule.

This process of ruling has been hidden from public attention by stressing the function of the government in governing. This device is useful in that the destitution imposed by the elite can be blamed on this or that government, who can simply be replaced during the next electoral circus.

While parliamentary elections can diffuse much social discontent, there are those who seek a more radical stance by opposing Parliament itself. With such slogans as 'Whoever you vote for the Government gets in', 'If voting could change anything it would be made illegal', and 'Guy Fawkes was the only person to enter parliament with honest intentions', anarchists have participated in the charade they profess to despise. The worst product of parliamentarianism is anti-parliamentarianism. While parliament is concerned simply with government, the ruling class's power rests on its ability to rule.

LINES OF POWER?

If we trace the roots of the meaning of rule we find ourselves led back to ancient Sanskrit. Nigel Pennick and Paul Devereux discuss this in their book *Lines on the Landscape: Leys and*

Other Linear Enigmas (Robert Hale, London, 1989). Using the work of Jim Kimmis they show how modern words like rule, *roi* ('king' in French), *Reich* ('empire' in German) etc. are tied to older words such as *rex* ('king' in Latin), *rîg* ('king' in Old Celtic) and also words meaning straight – *riht* (Old English), *reht* (Old High German), *rectus* (Latin). Of course rule and ruler in modern English also denotes drawing a straight line. These roots are also linked to the Hindi word *raj*, which means 'rule'.

Pennick and Devereux cite the ritual procession of Winchester College up St Catherine's Hill as an example of 'straight walking traditions' (see our booklet *The Great Conjunction* for a more detailed analysis of this), and then speculate as to how the king embodies a 'supernatural' power with transmission lines enabling 'the king's spirit to radiate out through the kingdom' – maintaining a form of occult rule combining 'order, power, government and the Earth Spirit itself'.

Nevertheless, they do not take up the sense of right as the opposite of left. Asger Jorn pointed out (*Open Creation and its Enemies . . .*, English translation, second edition, Unpopular Books, London, 1994) how *droite* (right) is connected with ascension, with rationality and justice, while the left is 'by nature the anarchic direction of the game'. However, Michael Dames has pointed out how right and left are differentiated in the northern hemisphere by the passage of the sun over the right shoulder for an observer facing the rising sun in the east. Thus right comes to represent solar power, and left a hidden process that defies reason but nevertheless restores the sun to its initial position at sunrise.

Despite their calls for harmony from *The Ancient Science of Geomancy: Man in Harmony with the Earth* (Thames & Hudson, London, 1979) to *Earth Memory: The Holistic Earth Mysteries Approach to Decoding Ancient Sacred Sites* (Quantum, London, 1991), Pennick and Devereux refuse to deal with the clear fact that there can be no move towards harmony without social revolution. As Asger Jorn put it: 'The battle of the upper class against the dragon and the serpent is not simply the battle against nature, but the battle against man's own nature, the battle against fortune and luck' ('Apollo or Dionysus', cited in Graham Birtwistle, *Living Art: Asger Jorn's Comprehensive Theory of Art between Helhesten and Cobra (1946–1949)*, Reflex, Utrecht, 1986).

THE SCARLET WOMAN AT GREENWICH

In our previous issue we highlighted the Queen's involvement in an act of ruling – visiting Greenwich, one of the most important sites in Britain, during an eclipse. The scarlet clad Queen entered the Masonic temple along a prime ley line, and crossed the very spot where Sir Walter Raleigh threw down his cloak for her namesake. Then the 'scarlet woman' reviewed the massed ranks of the Royal Hospital School, many of whom openly displayed rifles and sub-machine guns.

In the end it coincided with the investiture of Nelson Mandela, and her husband, the Baron of Greenwich, was unable to attend as he was in Africa. One of Mandela's first actions was to apply to rejoin the Queen's commonwealth.

First published in the *London Psychogeographical Association Newsletter* 7, Lughnassadh 1994.

CONTRIBUTIONS TO THE EVOLUTIONARY STRUGGLE INTENDED TO BE DISCUSSED, CORRECTED AND PRINCIPALLY PUT INTO PRACTICE WITHOUT DELAY

Inner City AAA

The days of this society are numbered. Its reasons and its merits have been weighed in the balance and found wanting; its inhabitants are divided into two parties, one of which wants to build their own spaceships and leave this society behind. A Five Year Plan for establishing local, community-based AAA groups around the world, dedicated to building their own spaceships, is part of the AAA's independent space-exploration programme, launched on 23 April 1995. The AAA released balloons into the air at 3 p.m. (GMT) in synchronisation with Autonomous Astronauts across the world doing likewise in celebration of this historic occasion. Dream time is upon us . . .

Inner City AAA Mission Statements include these declarations: technology is developed by the military and intelligence agencies as a means of controlling their monopoly on space exploration; economic austerity is manufactured by the state to prevent the working class building their own spaceships; governments are incapable of organising successful space-exploration programmes. *What we need today is an independent space-exploration programme, one that is not restricted by military, scientific or corporate interests*. An independent space-exploration programme represents the struggle for emancipatory applications of technology.

Whilst NASA refuse to conduct any research into sex in space, the AAA intend to openly explore sexual possibilities in zero gravity. Already Inner City AAA is designing several experiments that we wish to conduct to test our hypothesis that sex in space will be lots more fun. However, whilst we *will* undertake these experiments, we want to stress that the improved quality of sex in space is not the only reason to build spaceships. The media has attempted to concentrate its gaze on this aspect of our programme, but they have obviously yet to realise that we may also choose to use the promise of sexual experimentation as a promotional ploy to further our own ends. The year 2000 is right around the corner . . .

All too often, those in opposition to the current government, military and corporate monopoly on space exploration fail to set themselves realistic goals. And all too often this failure, this lack of a structured and disciplined plan of action for obtaining independent space exploration, leads to cynicism, despair, defeatism and, in some cases, insanity. The Association of Autonomous Astronauts knows that to achieve our goals we must firstly understand the terrain we are playing on. So our Five Year Plan emphasises the need for rigorous training. However, unlike our enemies at NASA we do not concentrate on physical capabilities, scientific careerism or military brainwashing.

Autonomous Astronauts must think for themselves. This is why the Association of Autonomous Astronauts researches skills that use the imagination, requiring the ability to move in several directions at once, exploring the power to abolish thought constructs we are commonly socialised into believing, like, for example, the concepts of space and time. Playing three-sided football has been a crucial component to training at Inner City AAA, who reports that it improves competence in deception, even preparing players for learning how to change and adapt the terrain they play on.

The Five Year Plan also emphasises the need for spreading a diversity of ideas about space travel. Through a world-wide network of groups dedicated to developing their own independent space-exploration programmes, ideas collide with each other and new possibilities are made available. Unlike the bureaucratic structures of government space agencies, the Association of Autonomous Astronauts grows laterally, branching out in several directions at once. We understand that, to achieve our goals, the form that we organise in and the way we connect to each other are as important, perhaps more important, than the propaganda we produce.

Creating a critical distance between ourselves and our space-exploration projects is another important element to the Five Year Plan. Autonomous Astronauts are constantly questioning what they are doing, looking at space travel from new angles, considering other possibilities and directions to move in. Only by doing this can Autonomous Astronauts avoid the pitfall of basing their identity on being space explorers. We must be ourselves first and foremost, and Autonomous Astronauts only after that. If identity becomes cemented to the process of Autonomous Astronauts struggling to develop independent space-exploration programmes, how soon before these Autonomous Astronauts inherit a vested interest in maintaining the status-quo?

The Association of Autonomous Astronauts recognises that to fully achieve our goals we may well have to entirely reinvent current attitudes to space travel. But Inner City AAA is confident that the Five Year Plan, which emphasises structured and disciplined projects, realistic short-term goals, rigorous training, a world-wide network and the constantly revised critical distance between ourselves and our space programmes, will be enough to change minds. Only those who attempt the impossible will achieve the absurd.

It is an appropriate moment to consider some of the responses made so far to the Association of Autonomous Astronauts' Five Year Plan for establishing a world-wide network of independent and community-based space-exploration programmes.

There have been small-minded idiots working in various arms of the media industry who attempt to denigrate our efforts and pass them off as being completely ludicrous. For example, *The James Whale Show* rejected us at the last moment on the grounds that we would be too esoteric for their audience. These responses always dispute the possibility of us achieving our goals because of the vast amount of money that must surely be required. Our reaction to this evident lack of imagination is composed of several levels. We can patiently remind these buffoons that an evolutionary impetus cannot be prevented from fulfilling what it pursues; after all, the dreams of those who desire to doubt everything transform the world. We can also suggest that reinventing current attitudes to space travel may well demand a total redistribution of resources throughout society, and that, in any case, some forms of space travel may well turn out to be surprisingly cheap. Again, the point is, of course, that only those who attempt the impossible will achieve the absurd.

There are those sad fools who proclaim their opposition to all forms of oppression but then ridicule the AAA's activities because we don't deal with 'reality'. As if they can stand in judgement over us and pronounce what is and is not to be considered as 'reality'. The AAA can show these imbeciles how we are in control of our own 'realities': by creating independent space programmes and building our own spaceships. We do not need anyone to tell us what can and cannot be thought, experienced, dreamt of, etc. After all, we have learned to travel in space.

And then come those packs of intellectuals, the twits who consider themselves so clever just because they can detect some subliminal advertising, and who tell us in extremely patronising tones how they can appreciate our endeavours as a form of serious joke or, even worse, as a metaphor for other struggles. These twats proudly inform us, as if they've just completed another crossword puzzle, how great it is that we are creating a living myth that anyone can participate in. Surely nothing but contempt should be spared for these slimeballs, so full of themselves they remain oblivious to the efforts of the AAA as we achieve definite results, prepared to put our theories into practice.

The AAA will not be pigeonholed and adopt a fixed agenda, or pinpointed to any single ideology. The AAA moves in several directions at once, using our own well-placed contradictions. The evolution will come because of the infiltration of clear and articulate language into the area of human space exploration. As a response to the present situation of government, military and corporate control of space travel, the AAA represents that evolution.

First published in *Here Comes Everybody! The First Annual Report of the Association of Autonomous Astronauts,* London, April 1996.

BEYOND CHAOS, BEYOND COHERENCE

Luther Blissett

I

That desire should stand head and shoulders above all other mystifications as the most spectacularly effective agent of recuperation in our benighted epoch is the most sickeningly predictable achievement of a principle whose destruction has been the cornerstone of every half-baked orthodoxy from Buddhism to Christianity. With the disintegration of all religious systems in the eighteenth century, the means by which desire was foisted upon the human body underwent a dialectical inversion, enabling the rising bourgeois class to increase the repressive potential of this principle. Desire ceased to be a temptation that, if indulged, led to suffering and/or damnation. Instead, it became an agent of the much-vaunted gratifications of an illusory future against whose promises the actuality of the present is to be permanently deferred. Accordingly, the present is now rationally organised around the (future) fulfilment of desire. The success of this racket accounts for capital's apparent 'escape'. After two centuries in which to assimilate these facts, only an imbecile would stand up and wail about the continual domination of the past over the present (original sin). And, as if to prove their own idiocy, the self-styled (anti-) militants of the (ultra-)left continue to babble about the end of history. It should be patently obvious to everyone that, under capitalism, desire acts as the central mechanism by which a non-existent future dominates not only the present but the past as well.

That desire should be held up as a 'revolutionary' principle by everyone from bedsit intellectuals such as 'the Pleasure Tendency' (whose name is sufficient to demonstrate the poverty of their theoretical practice) to the softest of the soft cops 'schizoanalysising' us with so-called 'anti-psychiatry', serves to make patently obvious the distance between the proletarian movement and all ideologists.

Anyone who promotes the confusion of desire and sexuality, and then reifies this dichotomy into an acceptance of the separation between the present and life, stands in opposition to the revolutionary movement. Desire is the commodified form of sexual (non-)relations. It is material proof of separation under capital, the principle by which the poverty and dissatisfactions of daily life are passed off as a 'natural' and 'universal' given.

II

When a group of self-styled 'radicals' such as 'the Pleasure Tendency' define 'art' as 'the commodity form of creativity' (*Desire Value and the Pleasure Tendency*, The Pleasure Tendency, Leeds, 1985), they pave the way for the reform of capital rather than its abolition. Art is any artefact, or even idea (conceptual art), packaged and sold as an expression of human values, the human spirit, the human condition, etc. That art is valued economically is true enough, but what witless leftists such as the Pleasure Tendency fail to understand is that 'art' is valued economically precisely because of the creativity (labour) put into it.

Creativity is labour raised to moral good; it lends credibility to the ridiculous notion that there is a 'universal' human need for 'expression'. The concept of creativity is just as repressive, moralistic and alienated as that of 'art'. That creativity should be held as the highest goal of human 'life' by self-styled 'revolutionaries' demonstrates the vast gulf between wannabe leaders and the impossible class.

III

The idea that wo/man is somehow separated from nature is typical of the lies and anti-dialectical inversions propagated by apologists for the imagination. Nature does not exist somewhere outside us; it is a social construction, the BIG LIE propagated by so-called 'creative' wo/men. For wo/men to build cities is as natural as birds building nests. If 'urban' environments are unnatural, then so are the lairs and burrows of other mammals. Bourgeois ideologists present our separation from 'nature' as a 'natural' fact that mirrors and explains all the social separations we suffer under capital. However, bourgeois ideologists cannot present us with the date at which our separation from nature occurred because the very idea of 'nature' is a monstrous fabrication. Ecology is the ultimate 'human' ideology. Green politics are based on notions of balance whose basic premises are drawn from the dualities induced by social separation. Ecologist equate change (which is inevitable) with destruction (a relative concept). Only a society fractured to its very core by capitalist social relations would allow concern about the 'future' (the 'desire' to be immortal) to dominate the present (life).

First published in *Smile 9*, London, 1986.

LUTHER BLISSETT THREE-SIDED FOOTBALL LEAGUE

London Psychogeographical Association

It appears that the first person to come up with the idea of three-sided football was Asger Jorn, who saw it as a means of conveying his notion of triolectics – a trinitarian supercession of the binary structure of dialectics. We are still trying to discover if there were any actual games organised by him. Before the LPA organised its first game at the Glasgow Anarchist Summer School in 1993, there is little evidence of any games being played.

There is, of course, the rumour that Luther Blissett organised an informal league of youth clubs which played three-sided football during his stint at Watford in the early eighties. Unfortunately, our research has found no evidence to support this. Nevertheless, Blissett's name will probably remain firmly linked to the three-sided version of the game, even if in an apocryphal fashion.

The key to the game is that it does not foster aggression or competitiveness. Unlike two-sided football, no team keeps a record of the number of goals they score. However they do keep a tally of the goals they concede, and the winner is determined as the team that concedes fewest goals. The game deconstructs the mythic bipolar structure of conventional football, where an us-and-them struggle mediated by the referee mimics the way the media and the state pose themselves as 'neutral' elements in the class struggle. Likewise, it is no psychosexual drama of the fuckers and the fucked – the possibilities are greatly expanded!

The pitch is hexagonal, each team being assigned two opposite sides for bureaucratical purposes should the ball be kicked out of play. The blank side is called the frontside. The side containing the orifice is called the backside, and the orifice is called a goal. Should the ball be thrust through a team's orifice, the team is deemed to have conceded a goal – so in an emblematic fashion this perpetuates the anal-retentive homophobic techniques of conventional football whereby homoerotic tension is built up, only to be sublimated and repressed.

However, the triolectic appropriation of this technique dissolves the homoerotic/homophobic bipolarity, as a successful attack will generally imply co-operation with the third team. This should overcome the prominent resistance to women taking their full part in football. Meanwhile the penetration of the defence by two opposing teams imposes upon the defence the task of counterbalancing their disadvantage in numbers through sowing the seeds of discord in an alliance that can only be temporary. This will be achieved through exhortation, body language, and an ability to manoeuvre the ball and players into such a position that one opposing team will realise that its interests are better served by breaking off the attack and allying themselves with the defending team. Bearing in mind that such a decision will not necessarily be immediate, a team may well find itself split between two alliances. Such a situation opens them up to the possibility of their enemies uniting, making maximum use of this confusion. Three-sided football is a game of skill, persuasion and psycho-geography.

When the ball goes out of play on the frontside, a throw-in is conceded. This is carried out by the team whose frontside it is, unless they had last touch. In that case the throw in is taken by the team whose goal is the nearest. When the ball goes out of play at the backside, the defending team has a goal kick, unless they had last touch, in which case a corner is taken by the team whose goal is nearest. The semicircle around the goal functions as a penalty area, and it may be necessary to use it for some sort of offside rule that has yet to be developed. The LPA has set up the Luther Blissett Three-sided Football League (LB3FL) and would like to hear from people interested in playing three-sided football.

First published in *Fatuous Times* 4, London, 1995.

CAER RUIS

The 'Empty Chair' of the Isle of Dogs

Preliminary Committee for the Founding of a New Lettrist International

The dissolution of ancient ideas goes hand in hand with the dissolution of ancient conditions of existence.

In order to facilitate the founding of a New Lettrist International, the Preliminary Committee has seen fit to inaugurate the Bardic Chair of Caer Ruis, to be located on the Isle of Dogs. In so doing we open an amplic phase of our activity. Located in East London, this beautiful arbour is a haven of peace and quiet amidst all the hurly-burly. Located right by the Mudchute DLR station, and in sight of Canary Wharf, it is well worth a visit next time you're in the area. Despite the despoliation of much of the Isle of Dogs by a predatory capitalism, the Elder Grove of the Mudchute remains. This grove is located along the western side of the earthwork thrown up in the development of the Millwall Dock. It was laid out like an Iron Age hillfort, until a supermarket was built in one corner. The Greenwich ley line passes through the northwest corner of the grove.

According to the Celtic letter system, each letter is associated with a tree, and Ruis has the elder assigned to it. This letter is the last letter, and governs the period from 25 November to 22 December. Under the old system ($13 \times 28 = 364$ days $+ 1 = 23$ December), Ruis gave way to the day of renewal. Walter Tyrrell stood under an elder tree when he loosed the shaft that did away with William Rufus. Yet under the Anglo-Saxon runic Futhark system, the elder is associated with the first letter Feoh, and assigned a period beginning on 29 June through till 14 July. It is also linked with cattle, which constituted the alienable wealth of these people. The elder thus constitutes an Alpha and Omega, the close of the British system and the opening of the Anglo-Saxon period.

However Feoh is in turn linked with the Nordic Goddess Freya, from whom Queen Elizabeth II claims descent through her Norman lineage (William the Bastard). She and her clan have shown an unhealthy interest in the Isle of Dogs, whether it was the clandestine meeting between the Duke and Duchess of York, or the more recent Prince of Wales Trust performance broadcast on Boxing Day. During the Prince of Wales broadcast orchestrated by Jonathan Dimbleby, the inhabitants were subjected to a simultaneous firework show from the royal ship Britannia. This was conducted precisely during that part of the programme when Charles whinged pathetically about why he wants a boat to play with.

Our decision in naming this Bardic Chair Caer Ruis, with no reference to Feoh, was made after deep deliberation. We are as much out of sympathy with any Celtic 'ethno-particularism' as we are with that which permeates radical (i.e. rooted) Anglo-Saxon culture. Our decision was based on aesthetics, and the Feoh rune has too many associations with the Windsor gang. Finally, from our surveys of the locality, we feel midwinter more appropriate. We have also decided to maintain Caer Ruis as an Empty Chair in order to express our abhorrence with the dominant social powers. This act of negation makes the seat much more powerful than if someone had felt up to assuming it. Aside from obliquely criticising the tendency of many Druidic orders to set up Bardic seats without properly considering whether they are worthy of such a role, we see this as an assertion of the power of negative thinking.

It is our proposed aim and ambition to celebrate Caer Ruis in August 1997, on the exact 400th anniversary of the play The Isle of Dogs being suppressed. Of its authors, Thomas

Nashe fled, while Ben Jonson was thrown in gaol. Jonson was described as the last of the Chief Poets by Robert Graves in his book *The White Goddess*.

First issued as a leaflet, London, 1995.

BAN MACBETH

Campaign to Abolish the Complete Works of William Shakespeare

We call upon the government to take immediate action to ban this evil play and all other works by the depraved author William Shakespeare. It is our desire to see these foul abominations publicly burned as a warning to others. The public will no longer tolerate the vomit that is thrust down our throats that some call culture, art and literature.

It has been revealed that *MacBeth*, the sadistic work of sixteenth century playwright William Shakespeare, was the favourite book of Stephen Wilkinson, the fucked-up-schizo-psycho-killer who viciously stabbed to death a defenceless twelve-year-old schoolgirl last March. Schizo-Wilkinson carried a copy of *MacBeth* with him everywhere and tragically so on that fatal day last March when he marched into Halgarth Comprehensive School in Middlesborough carrying in his holdall three knives, a hatchet, a Colt 45 replica revolver and a copy of *MacBeth*. It has also been revealed that Wilkinson had pinned a quotation by Jonathan Swift to his bedroom wall, describing humanity as a 'pernicious race of little odious vermin'. From this evidence we believe that it is not far-fetched to draw the conclusion that Wilkinson's reading of these black mass-terpieces of the occult led directly to the brutal murder of the innocent young schoolgirl.

This is evidence enough in our eyes that *MacBeth*, and other works by William Shakespeare reported to contain many depraved acts of sex and violence, be removed from the national curriculum forthwith and that the poisoning of our children's young minds ceases immediately.

Who knows what other works by Shakespeare (that freak of nature some call a writer) psychos like Wilkinson could have read and what disgusting filth is pillaging our children's innocent young minds. The works of these shameless authors litter our bookshops, which in some cases are no more than brothels. How can we defend publication and distribution of this noxious material? Those responsible should be prosecuted and punished. We will not rest until William Shakespeare's works are banned and banned for ever; then and only then will we sleep safely in our beds. We await the government's response.

First issued as a leaflet, *Shakespeare is a Sicko*, by the Campaign to Abolish the Complete Works of William Shakespeare, Glasgow, 1996.

THE GRAIL UNVEILED

Neoist Alliance

Much of the 'critical' writing on the subject of the Grail contains banalities about asking the 'right' question. In various Grail legends the widow's son brings disaster upon his people by failing to pose a specific query and, as a direct consequence, vegetation withers and castles crumble to dust. Reactionary commentators such as Anna Morduch in *The Sovereign Adventure: The Grail of Mankind* (James Clarke, Cambridge and London 1970) suggest that two types of question are asked about the Grail. The first is: 'Who serves the Grail? What is its nature? How can I serve it?' According to Morduch, the other type of questioner asks for the 'gifts and rewards' of the Grail. Naturally, these two formulations elicit different replies. In fact, those who wish to serve the Grail restrict themselves to asking absurd rhetorical questions about this world. These creeps are incapable of breaking the bonds that enchain them because they earnestly desire to serve the powers that be. The second type of questioner makes the same assumptions as the most 'noble' Knight of the Grail, but asks for grace and favour instead of offering service, and in doing so breaks the code of chivalry. In the past, such wretched creatures knew only banishment and exile, whereas today they're thrown a few crumbs of charity.

In the opening pages of *The Ego and its Own,* written 150 years ago, Max Stirner banished the spooks that Morduch attempts to conjure up:

What is supposed to be my concern! First and foremost, the

Good Cause, then God's cause, the cause of mankind, of truth, of freedom, of humanity, of justice; further, the cause of my people, my prince, my fatherland; finally even the cause of Mind, and a thousand other causes. Only my cause is never to be my concern. 'Shame on the egoist who thinks only of himself!' You have much profound information to give about God, and have for thousands of years 'searched the depths of Godhead', and looked into its heart, so that you can doubtless tell us how God himself attends to 'God's cause,' which we are called to serve . . .

Those of us who wish to see the castles of our oppressors crumble to dust, who are happy to watch feudal vegetation wither and die, and who would gleefully plough salt into these barren fields if that was what it took to set this process in motion, do not restrict ourselves to the dualistic system of 'thought' served up by Morduch. We are free to ask a question that has been posed many times before, a query that has a very simple answer. International best sellers such as *The Holy Blood and the Holy Grail* by Baigent, Leigh and Lincoln (Corgi, London, 1983) demonstrate that many people are still curious to know what the Grail is, or at least was or might have been. Baigent *et al.* suggest that the Grail is the blood of Christ which has been passed down among a direct line of his descendants. More traditional answers to the question of what the Grail is have included the cup that caught the blood from Christ's wounds as he bled on the cross, and a stone that fell from Satan's crown.

It is claimed that the Grail romances are a Christianised version of earlier Celtic legends, and that variants of these fables exist in all cultures. In *The White Goddess*, Robert Graves claimed that there is a true theme addressed by all poets, and that this can be found in its purest form among the works of the Celtic Bards. Graves doesn't understand poetry; it means 'genesis' or 'making'. As with poetry, so with the Grail. Nothing of consequence is learned by asking what the Grail was or might have been. What the Grail symbolised in past times is of no consequence to those who have broken with 'tradition'. In any case, tradition is itself discontinuous; individuals who wish to 'return' to tradition simultaneously break with the traditions they've inherited. This fact accounts both for the richness of Protestantism during its historical phase, when the influence of Islamic culture provided the driving force behind the Reformation, and for the utter poverty of nationalist ideology in our century.

Cultural cross-fertilisation is enriching and the Grail represents a historical accumulation of myths that cannot be collapsed into each other or 'restored' to the 'purity' of a 'Celtic' vegetation cult without being reduced to a one-dimensional banality. The power of the Grail legends lies in the fact that they are simultaneously Christian and Pagan, although this appears to have escaped the notice of the 'traditionalists' René Guenon and Julius Evola. The 'ideas' of the Catholic reactionary and former National Front activist Derek Holland are even more absurd. Influenced by Evola, Holland raves about the 'New Man' in his 'Political Soldier' pamphlets. It isn't clear whether or not Holland knows that the notion of the New Man is derived from the novel *What Is To Be Done* by the Russian 'nihilist' Nikolay Chernyshevsky. This book was in its turn heavily influenced by the utilitarianism of J.S. Mill, whom Chernyshevsky translated and whose thought was basically a secularised version of Islamic-cum-Protestant theology. Thus, in attempting to retrench Catholic traditionalism, Holland embraces not only the paganism of Evola, but also an extremely virulent strain of the Protestant 'heresy'.

The Grail can only be understood when it is viewed historically, that is to say as an unstable signifier of continuous becoming. On 20 February 1909 the Futurist F.T. Marinetti announced to a startled world that 'time and space died yesterday'. It was these words that ushered in the current epoch of avant-bardism. Likewise, it is said that the founder of the Ecole Druidique was Max Jacob – cubist, poet, critic, occultist, hoaxer and notorious blagueur. Druidry was (re)invented in the aftermath of the Renaissance as 'educated' opinion became divided over the relative merits of the Ancients and the Moderns. With the emergence of a dynamic conception of history, feudal dualisms were displaced by secular ideological wars such as that waged between 'progress' and 'tradition'. The modern 'revival' of Druidry is usually traced back to the election of John Toland as Chosen Chief in 1717, the very year in which the United Grand Lodge of Freemasonry was established in London!

The classical avant-garde in the form of Futurism, Dadaism and Surrealism emerged at the precise moment Aleister Crowley was reworking the Golden Dawn's remarkable synthesis of occult traditions, to create 'High Magick' as we know it today. Just as the avant-garde fakes its modernity, so Druidry fakes its antiquity. There is no evidence to suggest that contemporary pagan and esoteric 'traditions' pre-date the Renaissance. The avant-garde and the occult are two sides of the same coin. This state of affairs is left unreconciled, but at a higher level of disunity, in avant-bardism. In the ancient Celtic fables 'geis' was the prohibited thing; with the Christianisation of the Grail legends it is necessary to add a 't,' the letter that represents the cross, to 'geis'. It is by this means that we arrive at 'Geist,' a concept that is absolutely crucial to the Hegelian system of philosophy. 'Geist' is German for both mind and spirit.

It should go without saying that the average 'occultist' is a jerk who 'studies' the 'metaphysics' of magick precisely because s/he finds the works of Kant, Hegel and Marx too difficult to master. Readers who have not been initiated into the ranks of the Neoist Alliance, or its higher orders, may feel that they are being treated like fools, but then this is a thoroughly natural state of affairs given that the widow's son in the Grail romances is merely one among many representatives of this archetypal figure. The fool achieves wisdom through the ongoing process of becoming, that is to say in 'his' quest for the Grail. As the people of the Grail, the Celts are not a 'race' but proof, as if it were needed, that miscegenation is the creative principle at work in evolution. Noble Drew Ali allowed Celts to join his

Black Muslim religion in the twenties because he considered them to be Africans. As recently as 1992 this idea formed the thesis of the book *The Black Celts: An Ancient African Civilization in Ireland and Britain* by Ahmed Ali and Ibrahim Ali, who state quite explicitly that this culture became completely mixed with that of a later wave of Indo-European settlers. The discovery of Europe by the North American Iroquois Indians, whose landings in Iceland and Eire prompted various Viking chiefs to sail West, led to the highly developed tri-racial culture of the ancient Celts.

Just as urbanisation destroyed the sacred groves of the 'original' Druids, so the avant-bard will destroy any remaining 'aura' emanating from the fields of art and religion. Likewise, since within 'traditional' Celtic culture the letters of the alphabet correspond to different types of tree, so supporters of avant-bardism campaign for a new orthography in which any remaining traces of this convention are chiselled out of the English and Gaelic languages. Avant-bardists declare the letter 'e' to be particularly contemptible. The peoples of 'the West' are all Celts now, and those who accept this fact constitute an avant-bard of presence. Since the Grail is an unstable signifier of continuous becoming it necessarily functions as a symbol of cultural cross-fertilisation. Therefore, certain of our bearings, let us set out once again on an unending 'Quest'. Our first task is a complete merger with the rising culture of the Pacific Rim under the aegis of an International Disorder of Druid Councils. This is the 'reality' of L'Anti-Académie Anglais; since the English do not exist we won't bother to reinvent them. FORWARD TO A WORLD WITHOUT FRONTIERS!

First published in *Re:Action* 2, Summer Solstice 1995.

A JOURNEY FROM DUCIE BRIDGE TO ANGEL MEADOWS, VIA SCOTLAND

Number two in a series of urban explorations

BD

Old Manchester, to a new Manchester; a walk through a haunted past, raised, levelled and raised again, even in the drizzle resonating with the lives of countless thousands who crowded into the area stretching from St Chad's on Cheetham Hill Road to St Michael's on the brow of the meadow that overlooked the medieval town with its markets and crosses, collegiate church and closes. An open space in the seventeenth century, common land for grazing, no good for grain or oats until the fateful year of the Beast 1666 when it was sown with a host of the dead, victims of the Plague, reputedly over 40,000 of them. So many dead children they said, in the plague pit the wraiths of lost infants haunted the fields and gave the place its name, Angel Meadows, though if there were angels there I knew them not.

And so in the nineteenth century it came to pass that the meadows became engulfed and consumed by the slaves of Moloch and Mammon and a Dickensian stew was created, of ginnels and hovels, a warren of tenements so foul and filthy, crowded with the damned, that even today the name Angel Meadows causes a shudder to pass through those who had first-hand knowledge of its slums.

But what of our journey, fair stranger? What tales are there to tell now as we embark on our quest for the past that gave life to today? Dress yourself warmly for we near the Solstice and the rain that shed its tears on the dead weeps upon us now as we step from the Salford side unto the iron span that crosses the railway lines of Victoria's engineers and leads us into Manchester.

This is Ducie Bridge and it has stood there all my life and other lives before. Neither time nor the Condor Legions could blow away this lifeline that was erected in the 1840s to carry the populace of the two cities over the iron roads that bled the waterways dry. But where does our journey take us after crossing the bridge; how to invoke our communion with the past? Stand and gaze with awe at the first skyscraper this City spawned, the CIS Building, built with the untainted money of the Co-operative Wholesale Society in 1962, every inch of its concrete and glass a testimonial to the power of the Common People. Savour that fact that Jimi Hendrix bewitched and bemused an audience on the threshold of change in early 1967 with a display of guitar pyrotechnics in the dance hall that nestles in its bowels, and turn your eyes left to the continuation of Corporation Street and start your walk on the left-hand side passing the architecture of municipal benevolence enshrouded in sanitary dwellings and storage emporiums that have now magically metamorphosed into hotels for weary business travellers, until you arrive at Red Bank. Turn left again underneath the railway arches until you reach the first left, overlooking where the River Irk curves south before plunging into tunnels under Victoria.

Let your gaze pan again. To your right, an old factory, and beyond that, rubble. You are gazing upon Scotland. Yes Scotland. On the border of Cheetham Hill and the Irwell. Stand and close your eyes and hear the tramp of marching feet, and crackling of fires and the sound of flint on metal as claymores are sharpened, the chattering of Gaelic as the clans of Bonnie Prince Charlie's Jacobite Army camped in Manchester on their ill-fated march south to regain the throne from the upstart German rabble who wallow in their own filth even now.

There on the banks of the Irk the Young Pretender's army rested, and even now in the A to Z the area is marked Scotland. Not far by, in living memory, was McDonald's Fields, gone now, but not forgotten in song; it exists in the *Penguin Book of English Folksong* as 'At the Angel Inn in Manchester', a Jacobite song that takes us back on our journey, from the rebel Clansmen's halt to the thieves' kitchen of Angel Meadows. For this is where our journey will end, on Angel Street at the site of the Angel Inn, only a few minutes' walk from Scotland.

Turn your back on Scotland, fair pilgrim, turn your back and walk away from the stench and pollution that besmirch the air of a pathetic dream of freedom, turn your back on the ruins of Victorian commerce and retrace your steps to Aspin Street. Walk up there, then stop for a minute and listen. Can you hear them? The doomed and the damned that filled the streets you are about to tread?

What lies before us now? Alas more space for the curse of the twentieth century, the car. Yes, there on your right, a clapboard Berlin Wall with writing on it, proclaiming the hidden space behind 'Reserved Parking for Employees of the CIS', but walk towards the gate at the end of Angel Street and squint through the chink in its padlocked and shuttered doors and you can make out the flagstones of St Michael's Place, the home of the dead.

Yes, herein they lie buried, the 40,000 lost souls. Once it was flagged and revered. The church, St Michael's, was adjacent. Steps lead down. Tales were told, ghosts were seen. Now there is nothing except a steadfast refusal to do anything with the site other than park cars on it. Ninety years ago it was different. A bare knuckle fight to the death took place here, when 'Stumpy' and 'Bacup Billy' fought and died, spurred on by nothing more than a purse of free beer and the promise of infamous glory. Barefoot children gathered here to greet the great and good who ventured here to open charitable missions. Reverend ministers were sent to St Michael's because the locals were considered a greater challenge for conversion than the heathens of Africa or China. The police patrolled in pairs and concerned individuals travelled through the narrow, cramped streets disguised in old clothes and accompanied by guides.

You can stand now on the site of St Michael's Church, and the council have even provided a seat, but apart from the remains of the gate and the name, you'd never know how many sought refuge there. Turn your back on the plague pit and look across the remains of Angel Meadow. In front of you the desolate industrial spaces and railyards that replaced the tenements in the 1950s. Over on your right the final remaining buildings. Go back through the gateway and trace your way towards Ranters' Hill, up there on the end of New Mount Street. The hill, no longer on the official map, was the site of Civil War non-conformist revolution. Manchester, for all its sins, was a parliamentary town and the Diggers and Levellers who preached there spoke of a wondrous new Jerusalem to come at Zion's Trumpet call when Babylon's walls had fallen.

A huddle of buildings, old and new, remains between Style Street and Angel Street: the bonded tobacco warehouse and Charter Street Ragged School, the Harp and Shamrock (quench your thirst there if the Corporation vandals haven't closed it down). Go left out of the pub door, along New Mount Street and there at the end of your journey is Angel Street with St Michael's Square hidden from your view by the eyesore wall. Look left and swallow hard – if the plague don't get you the typhoid will, or the cholera, or any of the hundred symptoms of the disease of poverty – and imagine a time when the streets swarmed with people, ragamuffins and merchants, prostitutes and missionaries, Jacobites, Roundheads. This was the sink of the people forced to live on top of thousands of corpses. When it rained, so it is reported, bones came up from the earth, the only crop that would grow there.

And the Angel Inn, beloved of Charlie's tartan horde? It lives on, let us imagine, at the Rochdale Road end of Angel Street, in the form of the Beer House, the real ale establishment that stands there now. Finish your journey there, dear stranger, shake the rain from your coat, for one journey ends and another begins.

First published in *Manchester Area Psychogeographic* 2, January 1996.

INTERNATIONAL GRAVEDIGGERS MANIFESTO

International Gravediggers

1 The gravediggers of the world have spent too much time burying the martyrs to the people's cause. We have one grave left to dig, that of the state. That grave shall be the world and the people of the world shall dance upon the grave.

2 The gravediggers of the world shall not lift a spade, unless it is to dig this last grave.

3 The state shall be buried wherever it should appear; quietly at dawn under the frosty ground; with a funeral at midday under concrete and tarmac; with tears in the evening thrust into the mire.

4 The gravediggers assert that the state is dead, that the stench from the corpse makes breathing intolerable, our food tasteless, our eyes itchy. For the sake of our health it should be buried soon, before we die of intoxication.

5 The state is dead. Let there be no talk of ghosts or other fantasies.

This is our manifesto. We shall produce more detailed analysis later as regards the method of burial.

SPADES OF THE WORLD UNITE? YOU HAVE NOTHING TO LOSE BUT YOUR GRAVEDIGGERS.

Those subscribing to this document: B. Cubas, J. Longthorpe, S. Longthorpe, Y. Gluckstein, J. Garter, P. Wallace, L.

West, T. Gough, J. Fournier, E. Smith, J. O'Donnell, P. Shaw, F. Spitzel, N. Howard, G. Hulme, G. Durante.

I.G. Communiqué No.1.

This document was drafted at the first meeting of the International Gravediggers held on 20 February 1976 and circulated as a leaflet.

RALPH RUMNEY'S REVENGE AND OTHER SCAMS

An account of psychogeographical warfare in Venice during the 1995 Biennale

Luther Blissett

The futurists wanted to murder the moonlight and flood Venice. Today the target of these jibes is a ghost town. Rampant commodification and a soaring cost of living has halved the size of the indigenous population. The remodelling and standardisation of the town for the benefit of the tourist industry has resulted in many Venetians being exiled inland. Those who remain are treated as unpaid 'extras' in a never-ending show. Out of season the narrow streets are empty, leaving them sad and desolate, particularly at night. There are serious pollution problems and, as a result of the construction of a methane pipeline in the Venetian Gulf, the town is in danger of sinking into the sea.

The mayor Massimo Cacciari was once a Marxist but has now embraced Heidegger. He belongs to the Left Democratic Party, and, like politicians everywhere, runs with the hare and hunts with the hounds. Publicly, Cacciari denounces the conversion of Venice into a gigantic museum and talks of revitalising the city by organising international conventions, exhibitions, trade fairs and other spectacular mega-events. However, when opposition movements call for *real* festivals unpolluted by commerce, he ignores their demands. Venetian politicians are demagogues: they lament the decline of the town as a means of justifying their call for international capital to invest money in Venice! What they're really interested in is selling municipal properties to the bosses of the multinationals.

Throughout the twentieth century, Venice has been a focal point for radical criticism. Having been the target of so many avant-garde assaults, the town's 'fathers' were eventually compelled to recuperate criticism by admitting the avant-garde. Even the most truculent performance art now features in the once deeply conservative international Biennale of Contemporary Arts. Therefore, it was only natural that Luther Blissett should declare psychogeographical war on Venice. One night, during the first week of the Biennale, Luther covered the walls of the town with hundreds of psychogeographical stickers. The stickers were red with a white bi-directional arrow and a green inscription 'LUTHER BLISSETT – PSYCHOGEOGRAPHICAL WAY – JUNE–SEPTEMBER 1995: A GREAT PERFORMANCE'. Venice is ideally suited to labyrinthal drifts, and the bi-directional arrow did not point to any particular destination. What the stickers alluded to was the notion of the *dérive*. Late at night on 7 and 8 June, Blissett harangued drunks in taverns and clubs, exhorting them to gather in parties and follow the arrows on the psychogeographical stickers. The intention was to create a 'rendezvous with nobody'.

How many hours would pass before we met another Luther strolling the deserted streets? Where would we meet them and how were we to recognise them? To resolve the last question, we distributed visiting cards featuring Luther's androgynous face and the caption 'This ticket is valid for a seat at the front row of the apocalypse.' These drifts were codenamed 'Ralph Rumney's Revenge' to commemorate the expulsion of a recalcitrant Englishman from the Situationist International in 1958, after he failed to complete a psychogeographical survey of Venice in the time allotted to the task. The only person I met during my drift was an inebriated Scottish woman. It was four in the morning, we were both tired and I didn't understand her grumbled English. I was at a loss for a moment and felt myself heavy with centuries of bourgeois civilisation.

Disguised as a handsome young man, Luther went to the Giardini di Castello and handed out press packs to art critics and upper-class guests. The publicity material was printed on expensive coated board, emblazoned with the headline 'LOOTA – THE ART MONKEY'. Two awful scribblings and the logo 'LB – Liberty for the Beasts' constituted the front page. On the back there was the following text:

> In 1985 the Animal Liberation Front broke into the University of Pennsylvania laboratory where, for more than fifteen years, Dr Thomas Gennarelli had been conducting cruel experiments on cercopithecoids and other primates. The torture was a complete waste of money, beyond providing the US Health Office with an excuse for extorting $1 million a year from taxpayers. The ALF stole the notorious 'Gennarelli Tapes' and distributed them throughout the world. The experiments were stopped by the government when the scientists involved were unable to prove they fulfilled any useful purpose.
>
> Some chimpanzees, including Loota, were bought by Ronald Cohn's Gorilla Foundation. Loota was found to have an IQ of 80 (approximately that of Forrest Gump) and was taught to paint. A year after Loota's death, the Hans Ruesch Foundation is proud to exhibit his paintings. They illustrate the way in which beauty and intelligence are routinely butchered in the 'laboratories' of murderous pseudo-scientists. If Loota's head had been crushed in the name of 'research', we would not have the little treasures he painted before passing away peacefully in his sleep.

Inside, a fictitious Andreas Ruesch of Lugano was credited with authoring an exegesis of Loota's artworks:

> Loota represents nature as an archetypal world that counterbalances the painful memories of what he has been subjected to by humans. I look upon the thin blue lines of changing tonality meandering across the canvas (picture no. 16) as the outline of a mountain range. Perhaps the blot is an island – has Loota ever seen an island, or is this idea part

of the genetic heritage of his species? – which brings back memories of shining pebbles. Despite the terrible tortures he has survived, Loota's strange and secret alchemical art shows sympathy and optimism towards everything . . . The purple marks repeated and staggered in dark red (picture no. 4) on the ochreous background recalls the late Kandinsky . . .

The folder was also sent to many critics and faxed to the local and national newspapers. Everyone was invited to the opening of Loota's show at 6 p.m. on 10 July at the Foresteria Valdese. The ALF break-in, Gennarelli experiments, Gorilla Foundation and anti-vivisectionist activity of the Hans Ruesch Foundation were all real things and events, but this truth was simply a background against which the legend of Loota could be fabricated. Although Loota did not exist, a few months earlier there had been international press coverage of monkey paintings sold at an exhibition in Vienna. Many of the people who'd heard about these paintings assumed that Loota had produced them. Actually, 'Loota' was a corruption of 'Luther'. The local papers advertised the exhibition. Visitors arriving for the opening at the Foresteria were confronted by a leaflet. On one side there was a photograph of a banana, with its Chiquita logo replaced by Luther Blissett's face. The reverse side featured the following text:

Here is a picture. The pharmaceutical industry kills us while pretending to cure illness. The vast majority of the medicines they produce are either useless or actually harmful. They test their products on both people and animals. To respond to this situation with platitudes about 'animal rights' is grossly inadequate. The notion of rights is a product of bourgeois ideology and it is absurd to anthropomorphise animals. It is essential that we abandon all simplistic attitudes and back-to-nature romanticism. The fallacies of s-c-i-e-n-t-i-s-m which lead to laboratory experiments on animals must be defeated without recourse to anthropocentric bullshit about loving animals more than humans. The organic, anatomical, biological, metabolic, genetic and psychological differences between humans and all the other species are obvious and clear. Any objective observer can see that *no pharmacological or genetic tests are reliable.*

A sickness induced by unnatural and intrusive methods is fundamentally different from an illness 'spontaneously' arising inside an organism or provoked by a polluted but nevertheless 'uncontrolled' environment. *It is by arguments of this type that we can effectively defeat the vivisectionists. claiming that killing a macaco or a mandrill deprives the world of a potential artist simply reproduces the reigning ideology!* While public attention is focused on chimpanzee paintings, how many other primates are being massacred in labs without anyone giving a fuck about them? Self-styled 'animal liberation' ideologues like Peter Singer and Tom Regan only use moral arguments and pointedly ignore far more damning scientific evidence. These creeps haven't even won the moral debate; all they've succeeded in doing is deforming public opinion. There are plenty of people ready to visit an exhibition of monkey paintings without committing themselves to the struggle against iatrolatry. Likewise, vivisectors know that while 'animal libbers' restrict themselves to addressing moral issues, then their scientific deceptions will remain undetected. Funding for animal 'experiments' will continue to pour in as long as vivisectors can resort to bullshit about their 'ethical position' being predicated on saving human lives, while 'animal libbers only want to save dogs!' *Loota is just a product of my imagination, there is no painting here. Hans Ruesch knows nothing about this action; I've just made use of his address as a disguise, for he's a notorious anti-vivisectionist as well as one of the few you can trust.* You don't need any 'monkey art' to fight vivisection and all the other abuses of medical power! LUTHER BLISSETT, the animal liberation anti-artist'.

Various journalists stood aghast, unsure about what to write. A small child, whose parents had read about the exhibition in a local newspaper, began to cry when he realised there was no monkey. As a matter of fact, the papers failed to publish a key detail of Loota's story, his death. The father, who had taken his baby to the exhibition to see the monkey rather than to admire the paintings, gave me three or four unrepeatable epithets before leaving. He didn't give a damn about art or the Biennale; maybe he was the only decent fellow in Venice. Luther has the gift of ubiquity. While s/he was delivering the Loota flyer at the Giardini di Castello and the Lido, s/he simultaneously spread invitation cards for a *Virtual Self-Portraits* installation:

Virtual Self-Portraits – Interactive video installation
Enpleinair Gallery. Opening: Friday 9 June, 6 p.m.
Clairvoyants foresee the future in polished crystal spheres. In previous ages, the shamans of the Berber tribes achieved states of deep meditation simply by gazing at their own reflected image. It is a commonplace among many archaic cultures that a portrait imprisons the spirit of its subject. As a consequence, portraiture is forbidden and feared, or held in utmost respect. The historical origins of self-portraits melts into mystery and myth: the propitiatory shapes of huntsmen in Altamira, Narcissus seduced by his own reflection, and so on. The process and the medium of human sensorial perception are conditioned not only by natural laws but also by history. In literary fiction, it is the picture of Dorian Gray that decays with age instead of Gray himself. According to Duchamp, paintings die after a lapse of time in the same way as their authors, then they are placed in cemeteries, i.e. in the history of art. Located in the concrete space of a figurative discourse that constantly escapes itself, these Virtual Self-Portraits playfully expose the contradictions of this world. They are anonymous/universal, unique/manifold, ephemeral/persistent, immanent/transcendent, plagiarised/original, artistic/commoditised, etc.

If someone stares at a well defined image for a couple of minutes, the retina will retain an imprint of its outline. If the eyes are then focused on a white surface, a clear mental projection appears. This installation takes after-images as a starting point for the manipulation and projection of 'self-portraits'. The intention is to raise doubts by seducing the viewer into making deep and dark reflections on that paradigmatic feature of the post-modern age, the crisis of the subject. If it is true that the mental process is the only representative art of our time, personifying as it does the supercession of all mono-media parameters, then this installation may be compared to Alice In Wonderland's cake, which had to be apportioned before it was cut. Only the complete negation of the self-portrait can retain the authentic sense of such a discredited genre. VITTORE BARONI.

The piece above alluded to virtual reality without explicitly claiming any affiliation to it, in order to delude tourists into believing the installation was a hi-tech display. The Enpleinair Gallery did not exist: the name means 'open air', and the show took place in a normal courtyard. Visitors were confronted with a mirror that reflected virtual self-portraits of Luther Blissett, i.e. anyone who looked into it. As the curious moved away, their portrait vanished. Go ahead, cretin, there is room for all! The prank was explained with the following text:

The LUTHER BLISSETT project is open to all: anyone can look in the mirror and see LUTHER BLISSETT. The passers-by are LUTHER BLISSETT, everyone is LUTHER BLISSETT: my father, the Pope, Liala, Pasolini, Eluard, Fortunato Depero, Bui, Frank Zappa, Guy Debord, Kurt Schwitters, Oscar Wilde, Ray Johnson, Marlene Dietrich, Kerouac, Einstein, Man Ray, Mayakovsky, Pinot Gallizio, Duchamp, Harry Kipper, Keith Haring, Valentino, Fellini, Artaud, Che Guevara, Alberto Rizzi, Marilyn, Lennon, Piermario Ciani, Moana . . . It doesn't matter whether or not you consciously know it, even *you* are part of the LUTHER BLISSETT project. When you see LUTHER BLISSETT's face, you see yourself. This is the only *Virtual Self-Portrait* that will interest you! ALLEANZA NEOISTA, Venice, June 1995.

If Venice is the 'city of the spectacle', then we must reflect back at that city a pitiful image of itself. Our psychogeographical warfare was a success. More actions will follow shortly.

Loosely translated and abridged from Italian, first issued as an instant Internet classic in 1995.

NONSOLOGY WORKSHOP

Outer Spaceways Incorporated

In contradistinction to the rationalists who maintain that reason is the essential tool in the search for truth, and the irrationalists (e.g. Henri Bergson) who maintain that intuition is the essential tool in the search for truth, the nonsologist requires neither of these tools since s/he is not searching for truth, only nonsense. In this manner, liberation from such dubiosities as prejudice, boredom and elaborate schemata becomes a distinct possibility. Reality is composed of muchness of which there is much. It is not necessary to beat it into the shape of our language. We can let language turn into a flower. Let it bloom.

Every system of philosophy has been used to cast a veil over what is real, to the benefit of certain people in any society where it becomes prevalent. However, no system has yet been able to bury nonsense under its portentous statements, for nonsense has its roots in everyday experience. Change will result in society if people think more or think less.

Nonsense is a lever that can fragment the thought forms that have gradually solidified, thus preventing the free flow of thought which is not essential for anything. It just happens to be good, whatever that may happen to mean. Academic philosophy is very much an exercise in self-mutilation of the imagination. Academic philosophers are privileged to have their hobby financed by the rest of us, in other respects they are completely irrelevant and tiresome. If these intellectual insects were given apple-pie beds and coffee omelettes perhaps their horizons might be broadened. Cold baths are pointless, except perhaps in hot countries, e.g. Greece.

Shall we say:

- Only funny statements are true.
- Diogenes the Cynic.
- It's only life, it's real.
- It's all much of a muchness.

Why bother? It is a matter of choice. When entering an area with no rules it is wise to be careful; it is not necessary. Reason may be useful, but there is no guarantee. Total freedom leads to total responsibility; there are no cop-outs. I have no excuse for the cruddiness of this handout; it came about as reality unfolded itself.

NONSOLOGY DOESN'T NEED TO RULE – OK

Issued as a leaflet for a 1976 *Radical Philosophy* conference workshop.

THE FUTURE OF CRIME

Luther Blissett

In the 1960s a group of French radicals called the Situationists suggested that 'freedom is the crime that contains all other crimes'. Things have changed a lot since then, although those at the top of the social heap still believe that the vast masses of humanity are simply cattle to be fattened and slaughtered. It sounds like a cliché, but it's now ten years since 1984 and the hardware for our total electronic control not only exists, it is also completely obsolete.

The industrial economy based around railways, electricity and the car is a historical curiosity. Until recently, the technological innovations revolutionising society were centred on the generation, storage, processing and transmission of information. Today, we are witnessing the rise of a new technological revolution, a bioeconomy dependent upon genetic engineering, nanotechnology and neurocomputers. Obviously, the level of scientific, technological and cultural development within any given society dictates the types of crime that may be committed within it. Among nomadic tribes, the chief crimes are rape and murder. With the establishment of agriculture and the development of a class system, theft became the major concern of those who controlled the fast-expanding and increasingly bureaucratic legal system.

A lot of would-be trendy magazines and television programmes like to pretend they're covering the cutting edge of crime by running features on computer hacking. Basically, what these people present as the future of crime is hi-tech theft, with cybernauts ripping off money from bank accounts and credit card facilities. When you think about it, this scenario isn't so different from some farmer of three thousand years ago stealing his neighbour's cow. A theft is a theft is a theft, despite the fact that the methodology of larceny is transformed by technological developments.

What isn't being reported by the mainstream media is the way in which biotechnology, based on genetic engineering, is being used to boost the profits of multinational corporations as it simultaneously destroys the health of ordinary people. At its simplest, this consists of drugs such as Thalidomide being prescribed to pregnant women in Brazil, despite the fact that Thalidomide is banned in Europe because it causes children to be born without limbs. Biotechnology gets even sicker when it's combined with pre-existing forms of mind control based on psychiatric and electro-shock treatments.

While *RoboCop* and *Terminator* were presented to the public as futuristic scenarios, they portray a situation that already exists. The technology required to remake a man or woman, either psychologically or physically, has existed for years. This is where the future of crime really lies, because the police and intelligence services require criminal activity to keep them in a job. While biotechnology is being used to transform the bulk of the population into obedient slaves, the psychological aspect of such mass brainwashing works much more effectively when a minority of individuals are programmed to act as violent psychopaths. The passive majority already accept that the constant surveillance of both public places and cyberspace is fully justified to protect them from those maniacs who threaten the smooth functioning of a well-ordered society.

A huge body of publicly available literature exists on CIA experiments such as MK-Ultra, which used LSD as a means of turning ordinary men and women into mind-controlled zombies. A number of MK-Ultra test subjects were programmed to slaughter their fellow citizens. Everyone, from Luc Jouret and Charles Manson to Jim Jones and Mark Chapman (the bloke who murdered former Beatle John Lennon), is a victim of coercive psychiatry which transformed them from a regular guy into a murder maniac. During LSD sessions, these future killers were subjected to 'psychic driving', a torture technique that consists of revelations extracted under psycho-analysis being played back over and over again, via a helmet the victim can't remove. In the future, virtually every piece of mayhem to gain widespread publicity will be the involuntary act of some helpless sap whose murderous antics were pre-programmed in a government institution.

Alongside increasingly sophisticated mass-murder pro-grammes sponsored by the security services and multinational corporations, there will be resistance from those groups who have already been criminalised for wanting the freedom to party. The Criminal Justice Act, now in force, makes raves illegal and worse is to follow. Fortunately, there are still plenty of people about who want to defend themselves from this crackdown. In England, the resistance will be led by the London Psychogeographical Association, who will use games of three-sided football to free people from the shackles of dualistic thinking. Already, the state is preparing to outlaw football played on hexagonal pitches, with three goals, where a tally of the goals conceded reveals who has won. The shifting allegiances this game brings into play teaches people to break out of the dualistic system of thought that tricks them into becoming victims of the mind-control techniques employed by the ruling class.

When three-side football is banned, which will certainly happen in the next two or three years, the London Psycho-geographical Association will organise games in abandoned multi-storey car parks and the basements of deserted office blocks. Some games will be played for a full ninety minutes, while others will be broken up by the cops. Anyone arrested will have been told in advance to claim that they are Luther Blissett, a name which has been appearing mysteriously on buildings all over Bologna, Italy, in recent weeks. Some of those who are nicked during games of three-sided football will later reappear among their friends, and with great sadness they will be killed, to free them from the programming that's destroyed their personality and will compulsively drive them to murder anyone who resists the state. This is the future of crime and it demonstrates that the Situationists were right. FREEDOM IS THE CRIME THAT CONTAINS ALL OTHER CRIMES.

First published in *G-Spot* 14, Winter 1994.

THOMAS À BECKET

An English Imam?

London Psychogeographical Association

The Roman Catholic church calls him a saint and martyr, Aleister Crowley said he was a Druid – but in the middle ages it was a commonplace to say that Thomas à Becket was the son of a Syrian Princess. Many modern scholars follow the opinion of Sir John Watney, that this myth has no basis. To go along with an unsubstantiated opinion expressed by a top ideologist of the Mercers – the Numero Uno London Livery Company – is simply quite unacceptable.

Anselm Beckett's account *The Legend of the Chapel of St Thomas of Acon* is quite specific, even though it was written over two hundred years after the death of Thomas. Here, Thomas's mother bears the name Zuzima and is described as the daughter of Kaibal-Eddin, the Emir of Acre. Her tutors are given as Hadji-jazid and Abu-salu. The story recounts how she helped Thomas's father, Gilbert, escape from the Emir. Then she followed him to London, arriving just as he is about to marry another woman. The essence of the story is carried in the popular ballad *Lord Bateman*, where Becket's name gets changed to Beichan (and some derive the name Bacon from this), and Zuzima is called Sophia – perhaps the personification of wisdom.

THE CULT OF LOVE

The historian may dispute the truth of this legend, yet we must return to it presently. All agree, however, that Becket's mother was a major influence upon him as he developed a pious reverence for the Virgin Mary. His youth is littered with miracles – he narrowly avoided death when he fell in a mill race and a magic coverlet, when folded out, was too big to fit in that 'smooth place' known as Smithfield. Yet one myth concerning his career as a student in Paris is of particular relevance.

The Icelandic Saga of Archbishop Thomas gives an account of a student parliament 'whereat in a brawly wise each praiseth his own beloved'. When Thomas said nothing he was jeered and mocked, and called a lifeless mannikin. The following day each student was to bring a piece of needlework from his paramour. Thomas magically produced a full Bishop's rig from a beautiful ivory box, claiming that it was what his own beloved had brought the night before.

This second story is a reassertion of the traditional dualism of Christian thought – a perverted sensuality where 'woman' is elevated to an abstract principal but the physical presence of woman becomes the locus for the debasement of love as lust. Thomas indulged in a debased form of sensuality which involved wearing a hair shirt crawling with vermin. This is in stark comparison with the new poetics that were asserting themselves in Europe at this time. It originated in Muslim love poetry propagated by the Sufis. The Troubadours derived their name from the Arabic TRB = music, song.

In *Creative Mythology,* Joseph Campbell shows 'an unbroken, though variously modified, aristocratic tradition of mystically toned erotic lore, extending from India not only eastward as far as to Lady Murasaki's sentimental Fujiwara court in Kyoto, but westward into Europe, and even rising to almost simultaneous culmination all the way from Ireland to the Yellow Sea, at exactly the time of the calamitous adventure of Abelard and Heloise' – i.e. the time of Becket's birth.

Within the conventions of Sufi poetics, the story of Sophia's arrival in London can readily be interpreted as the transmission of Sufism (= sophia = knowledge) into an English environment.

A SUFI 'INVISIBLE COLLEGE'?

For those who appreciate the subtleties of Sufism, it will come as no surprise when we suggest that Thomas's sister Agnes might have been more important to the transmission of Sufism. Thomas had an unbalanced view of women and sexuality. This went hand in hand with his pursuit of a political career, which reached the highest positions in both state and church. Agnes harboured none of these ambitions. She did, however, found the Hospital of St Thomas, dedicated to her brother. This was based at their old house in Cheapside.

The question then arises: did this hospital constitute an 'invisible college' comparable to the Sufi orders of the Middle-East. The Hospital of St Thomas eventually became a military order like the better known Hospital of St John, or indeed the Templars. In fact, the Knights of St Thomas were very close to the Templars (there was great internal dissension about a proposed fusion with the Templars shortly before the latter were suppressed for heresy in 1307). The Knights of St Thomas had preceptories in Acre, Nicosia and Kilkenny, as well as London. By the fourteenth century, they had largely lost their military character.

The Hospital played a central role in hosting events for many London guilds. But the foremost guild, the Mercers, actually established their Hall within the hospital itself. Both the Merchant Staplers and the Merchant Adventurers established themselves as fraternities of St Thomas, and maintained very close links with the Mercers. At the time of their dissolution, the Master kept a 'cupboard of stages' amid the treasures in his sanctum. Among the various knick-knacks, the caskets of amber and gold, the Chinese and Japanese porcelain, the crystalline elephant, the ivory falcon, there was a collection of carved gourds brought from the New World.

ECLIPSE AND RE-EMERGENCE OF THE INVISIBLE COLLEGE

The Knights of St Thomas survived as a public body until the suppression of the monasteries by Henry VIII in 1537, whereon they hosted a 'last supper' attended by such people as William Cavendish, Robert Cecil and Venetian envoy Zamboni, along with representatives of the livery companies and the Hanseatic League. The Master of the Hospital (also referred to as a College by I.G. Clark in her 1865 edition of *The Legend of the Chapel of Thomas of Acon*), Laurence Gopferton made a speech referring to their 'illustrious predecessors of the chivalry of the Temple', as the grace-cup of Thomas à Becket was circulated. Gopferton made it clear that they would not resist their dissolution.

Sir Richard Gresham, Master of the Mistery of the Mercers, then rose to his feet and stated how it had long been his intention to ask the king's permission for the Mercers to take over the college's London premises, including the school that his son, later Sir Thomas Gresham, attended. 'The former teachers may thus continually abide. Nor shall the bond wherewith ye have bound our ancient brotherhood be lightly broken; nor in our keeping shall your church suffer decay; nor shall your portals be closed to the needy and the wayfarer; nor shall your good memory perish from this city; nor especially from ourselves, your familiars of the guild and mystery of mercers.' A monk responded that the dissolution was mitigated by such a proposal that could not fail to perpetuate their ancient seminary.

From this ancient seminary we can trace the emergence of this 'Invisible College' when Sir Thomas Gresham in his turn established Gresham College from which the Royal Society eventually emerged. When we find historic reference to the Invisible College, as in the letters of Robert Boyle, it is apparent that it is hardly invisible any more.

First published in *London Psychogeographical Association Newsletter* 8, Samhain 1994.

SHOPPING SPREES FOR THE PROLETARIAT

Decadent Action

Who wants to be a millionaire? . . . We do. Admit it, when it comes down to it, a big hunk of cash would enrich your life, wouldn't it? The 'underground' is full of people saying how terrible money and consumerism are, but they would sure as hell love a new computer or a photocopier to knock out their 'zine on. Maybe just a new pair of shoes or a winter coat would make things better. It's all a question of perception; after all it's not the produce that is wrong but rather the system of distribution, i.e. capitalism. Decadent Action offers a new and unique strategy to overthrow capitalism without the dour lentil-tinged guilt that surrounds the extreme left and anarchist groupings.

Decadent Action offers a plan based upon the principles that underpin capitalism itself, that is the simple equation of supply and demand. It is this equation that will decide the shape of 'the market' and hence the price of goods in the shops. One aspect of this relationship is the higher the demand the higher the price. This is a result of the rules of economics which state that there is a 'value' given to the goods based upon the scarcity of the resource. This can most simply be seen in the case of valuable gems and metals such as diamonds and gold. You are paying a high price because these are finite resources for which there is a high demand.

So the plan is this: we encourage everyone to spend as much as possible, and spend on luxury items too. This has a dual effect. First it encourages people to live outside their means and above their station. After all, why shouldn't you eat at the fanciest restaurant in town? Second, it is through buying that we can affect inflation. The main economic policy of this government is to control inflation through restriction of wage demands, high interest rates, and restricted growth of the economy. Full employment is an inflationary measure and simply does not make sense to a government wishing to run an effective economy

So get out on the streets, get yourself a credit card, maybe two or three, go wild in the aisles. Don't worry about the bills, we are talking about the collapse of the capitalist system here, crushed under it's own weight. The bills will become meaning-less trifles as we move into hyper-inflation somewhat akin to that of pre-war Germany.

Previously unpublished.

NEOISM AS NEGATION AND THE NEGATION OF NEOISM

Luther Blissett

There are many ways in which it's possible to explain the phenomenon of Neoism. A prosaic history of the movement would probably suggest that Neoism started life as No Ism, a concept invented during the late seventies by David Zack, Al Ackerman and Maris Kundzin in Portland, Oregon. No Ism was an open, inclusive and anti-ideological grouping of individuals who saw themselves as artists opposed to the gallery system. This idea was transmitted to a group of French Canadians via Istvan Kantor who'd fled Hungary on a student visa after David Zack enticed him to decamp to North America with the aid of some colour Xeroxes. Kiki Bonbon and the rest of the crowd Kantor befriended in Montreal then hit upon the idea of transforming No Ism into Neoism and parodying the legacy of the twentieth-century avant-garde.

The French Canadians had a gang mentality and Kantor found himself on the fringes of the group. Bonbon and his pals called their Hungarian friend 'grandpa' because he was in his early thirties. In an attempt to overcome his isolation, Kantor cultivated international contacts. Individuals such as tENTA-TIVELY a cONVENIENCE in Baltimore and Peter Below in Germany got involved with the group but Kantor remained a fringe figure who never fully understood the Neoist project. Kantor's cluelessness as to what was going on around him is legendary. Al Ackerman once told me that when Kantor arrived in Portland in 1978, the Hungarian was informed that a mentally retarded man who hung out with Zack would act as his manager and get his singing career off to a flying start. As the weeks passed, Kantor became increasingly abusive about the retard, regularly indulging in hysterical fits where he'd scream 'This guy is useless; he's supposed to be my manager but he hasn't got me any gigs.' Once he settled in Montreal, Kantor lived off the extremely generous Canadian grant system for the arts and established a reputation as a tame performance artist who was happy to work within the gallery system. In stark contrast to this, the bulk of the Neoist Network was made up of potential iconoclasts who spent much of their time challenging consensus reality. However, Kantor's convention-ality resulted in much of the press coverage the Neoists received during their early days focusing on him as an individual. Such verbiage now looks ridiculous – but rather than proceeding with a conventional interpretation of Neoism, I'm going to be more elliptical in my approach to the subject.

Allegorically, Neoism could be explained in the following fashion – during the middle ages there were a succession of heresies that have been described by the historian Norman Cohn as mystical anarchism. Adherents to these creeds believed that all goods should be held in common and that many things considered sinful by the Roman Catholic Church were in fact virtues when practised by the elect. Ranked among the more interesting of these sects are the Bohemian Adamites. On 21 October 1421, 400 trained soldiers moved against the Adamite heretics and virtually wiped them out. By a miracle, their leader – known both as 'Adam' and 'Moses' – escaped to Prague. 'Adam' then took on a disciple, who in his turn, trained up a further initiate after his master's death. In this way, the Adamite creed was passed down through the ages and the Neoist Network is simply a contemporary manifestation of this ancient heresy. Viewing Neoism through the prism of this alle-gory makes imagery associated with the group accessible to those who have not been initiated into its ranks. When the Neoists speak about Akademgorod as their 'promised land', this is actually a code name for Prague. According to Neoist eschatology, Prague is the omphalos of our planet and, once the movement seizes control of the city, the ancient Adamite plan of world domination will be effortlessly realised.

In keeping with this allegorical interpretation of Neoism, the initiation of individuals into the movement must necessarily be described as follows: the candidate is blindfolded and led into a darkened room. The fourteen secret masters of the world (or at least a group of available Neoists) interrogate the initiate. As a sign of obedience to the order, the candidate must answer 'yes' to a series of ninety-five questions. After this humiliating set-piece – in which the initiate admits to being a complete sexual failure – the candidate is fucked by every member of the lodge and then symbolically reborn by the removal of the blindfold. If this sounds an unlikely allegory, it's only because the story is – to an extent – literally true. John Fare was kept blindfolded for a period of seven days during the so called 'Millionth' Neoist Apartment Festival. During this time he was subjected to gropings and other sexual stimulations, made to carry dangerously sharp objects on the New York subway in the rush hour, had his usual sleep patterns completely disrupted, was flipped upside down and forced to run on his hands, etc.

Unfortunately, no one ever succeeded in ordering the rather loosely organised Neoist Network into a Masonic structure. Pete Horobin made a brave attempt with his Data Cell project but this operation was ultimately a failure. Of the various twentieth-century avant-garde movements, only the Surrealists and the Situationist International came anywhere close to replicating the classic structure of a secret society. Until 1984, Neoism was most obviously influenced by Futurism, Dada, Fluxus, Mail Art and Punk. I managed to forge a few links with the Situationist tradition after joining the group but my comrades lacked the discipline to make the most of this input. Ultimately, Neoism derives the little historical importance it can now claim from the fact that it acted as a false dawn prior to the organisation of the far more significant Plagiarist and Art Strike movements.

The Neoists wanted to avoid any single meaning being imposed on their activities and believed that by bombarding their movement with a series of contradictory interpretations they would split the meme and simultaneously create a monadic earthquake fierce enough to destroy world culture in its entirety. Thus Neoism was viewed simultaneously as modernist, post-modernist, an avant-garde transgression of modern and post-modern traditions, as underground, Neo-Dadaist and an outgrowth of Fluxus. It was also a rejection of all these things.

Like every other avant-garde group, the Neoists hoped to project an image of themselves as the very latest trend in culture and this accounts for the more archaic aspects of their project. The occult elements provided a perfect counterpoint to the movement's faddish innovations, making these appear even more newfangled and up-to-the-minute. It was a technique that had been employed very successfully by the Dadaists, Surrealists and Situationists.

Ultimately, the Neoist project was a failure because most of those involved with the group paid no heed to the lessons to be learnt from the critique of the image made by the Situationists and within Auto-Destructive Art. While the details of the Situationist theory are fatally flawed – partially due to Debord's obsession with the Stuart succession – the notion of the spectacle is still of some use to those who wish to break with the world as it is and create a new tomorrow.

The avant-garde is in many ways a return of the repressed, the re-emergence of Protestant iconoclasm in a post-Christian world where art serves as a secular religion justifying the activities of a murderous ruling class. For example, in 1441 Hugh Knight went into a Cornish church and burnt the chin off a statue of the Virgin Mary. The result was a work in which the Virgin appeared to have grown a beard, making this act of image-breaking an important precursor to Duchamp's moustached Mona Lisa.

The Specto-Situationist obsession with text is an inevitable result of the group's assault on the image. Guy Debord would have felt very much at home if he'd ever had the opportunity to hang out with the Bible-thumping Lollards of the Middle Ages. The word is sacred, idolatry (the dominance of the Spectacle) an everlasting sin. Before heaven is realised on earth and every wo/man can live in her/his own cathedral, the word must be accepted and the sensuous image stamped into the ground by a legion of jackbooted Debordists. The critique of the image made by Gustav Metzger, who used acid to simultaneously create and destroy 'auto-destructive' works, was a far more incisive response to Judaic, Islamic and Protestant traditions of iconoclasm than that of the Specto-Situationists.

While I remained within the Neoist Network, I was unable to synthesise these and other forms of contemporary iconoclasm. After breaking with Neoism, I announced the 1990 Art Strike, which brought together innumerable types of idol-breaking. Once I'd fashioned this coffin for the corpse of art and defiantly nailed my ninety-five theses to the lid, the Neoists realised they'd been decisively outflanked. It was at this point that they began to claim my post-Neoist activities as an integral part of their project.

Today, when a Neoist or one of their friends writes about the group, Luther Blissett becomes the chief star of the movement. Neoism is no longer an attempt at negation via the destruction of the meme. For the past five years, various ex-members of the group have attempted to claim successful examples of iconoclasm – such as the Art Strike – as being somehow related to their personal activities. And so, while Neoism is of no significance whatsoever and this is its most interesting attribute, the search for truth increasingly resembles a quest for an unholy grail. Although I split the meme in 1985, what actually matters is how long news of this achievement takes to spread among the various populations of the world.

Written for the forthcoming Creation Press publication *Negation: The Last Book*, edited by Jack Sergeant.

TELEVISION MAGICK

Thee Temple Ov Psychick Youth

TV AS MAGICK AND RELIGION

Is the deification and worship of technology an excusable response to the automation of human perception? During the Harmonic Convergence, one New Ager took a television set with her to the top of Mount Shasta, and then stunned the other observers by announcing that the image of an angel had manifested on the screen. The next day, before a large media conglomeration, a repairman re-activated the phenomenon and explained that it was due to a simple mechanical defect. Press and sceptics ate the story up with glee, but a pertinent point was missed. Who cares whether this videoised vision was caused by an other-worldly being, an unconscious group-will force or a shorted wire? Is not the human neurostructure, by which sensory data is received, but a complex system of wiring and basic automated processes? Spontaneous visual hallucination used to be a purely human characteristic.

The future utilisation of TV to transmit spiritual experience is an inevitable reality. Our all-encompassing environment, which used to be Nature, has become technology. Before Judeo-Christianity, all Western religions were quite under-standably based on the environment. Now that we have outgrown a flawed spiritual framework far removed from the principles of physical experience (and much worse as a result), why not return to a religion more direct, and in touch with the human condition? Because our environment is now self-created? Ah, but that is to be the hook of this new world-faith . . . Evolution is gracing us with the powers of Creation and Destruction we once projected out onto gods; or perhaps we are just realising them, latent within our psyches, the restless energies responsible for the seed of all spiritual thought . . . And so the medium is, indeed, the message.

Through these information and communication technologies, humanity has taken its most subjective inner experiences and offered them up, replicated, into the mass 'meme pool' of perceptual stimuli. In doing so we have structured a Gestalt of human reality, partially bridging the vast chasms between each universe of consciousness commonly know as 'a person'. Actually, we have re-created (in its own image . . .) the Gestalt for accepting either the spiritual notion of ultimate Unity, or the quantum energy grid of modern physics. We are beyond temporal impressions; all one Network of Being. In other words, we have unconsciously, but faithfully, fulfilled (in our own little way) the creative principle within us by embodying its essence and carrying it forth. In one respect, TV sets and hi-fi stereos have accomplished in a few years what organised religion has been striving towards for thousands.

Imagine a video tarot – workable as soon as the technology of 'shuffling' separate sequences is available (the CD-video). How many more corresponding attributions and possibilities for subjective impressions will be instantly at our grasp in a short video-effects segment than in a small playing card? Imagine TV ritual (Virtual Reality?). The point of ceremony in spiritual traditions, exo- and esoteric, is to trigger the inner experience through extraordinary sensory input. The potential of today's visual media for revolutionising this ancient transformative art, their technical advances making possible both the creation of virtually any image – and their accessibility to anyone – is obvious. And, of course, the technology will only improve, forging new pathways . . .

It is true that these communication systems are, for the most part, effecting today, the polar opposites of enlightenment. This condition has, however, provided some rare opportunities. Televisions are incredibly prolific. Most of the population watches them for long periods of time. From an evolutionary perspective this can be seen as an 'easing in' to a more vital project. Today's 'living room' has become a TV viewing room, as is evident by the placement of the set and the rest of the furniture in relation to it: an objective observer would probably assume that these devices already fulfil a religious function. The notion of 'TV as altar' is not new, but once again becomes relevant. We enshrine our video consoles the way we used to enshrine our god-images . . .

In the cathode ray, then, may be the Channel we must find. A true Network to tune in, the remote control of an infinite, viewing its illusory passion plays on a plane of static radiation – are we the image on the screen?

TV SNOW

Here television's application as a type of subconscious mirror for scrying is exposed. This type of working, as well as its use in cut-ups, were the main ideas that were submitted in the collation of this project. There is much more to be explored . . .

An important task in contemporary magick is redefining psychick uses of existing structures. Seemingly abandoned locations such as TV snow can be taken over and used by the magician. A Psychick Graffiti Zone. Infiltrate community channels, using night-time filler shows: one consisting of a camera taking a complete journey on a subway train could be salvaged for use in ritual.

The impression I get from TV snow images is that they may form a consistent language with a specific vocabulary of images due to the limited parameters of TV (as opposed to the structures of dreams) and the repetitiveness of the images. Are these images the same to people in completely different circumstances?

Basically, what I do is tune into a non-broadcasting channel and stare at the 'snow', trying to look at one point, usually near the centre of the screen. After a time, moving patterns start to emerge from the 'snow', like spinning mandalas, or large colonies of black ants dancing circuitously into their burrow . . . eventually I being to see several layers of things going on behind this . . . I can focus on any one layer, but not for long. There is so much information, it's rather like watching five or six films projected on top of each other (in layers) and trying to select one film to focus on. I can see topographical landscapes going by very quickly, as if flying over a continent. Deserts and sparse vegetation seem to be prevalent. Also scenes from everyday life: houses, people, cars, etc.

Groups of people dancing and twirling, columns of marching men . . . it's very similar to the Dreamachine, but with the eyes open. To stop all the images, all I have to do is re-focus my eyes on some other part of the room . . . Heavily amplified TV audio static seems to be a particularly enriched form of white noise (all frequencies combined). Audio-hallucinations can become quite complex – the audio equivalent of TV snow.

AMBIENT TELEVISION

If television has a unique ability to penetrate our subconscious, how can the individual regain control over it? One solution is to render it trivial. Things are most easily trivialised through such frequent repetition that they become commonplace. A television left on long enough becomes furniture, not entertainment! Stacks of TVs all tuned in to a different channel make it impossible to concentrate on a single linear programme; one's eyes roam from set to set. And this with as few as three sets.

IMAGE TRIPLED

The constant flickering image, constantly changing. The magick moments, when captured, can be visually stimulating. When stared into, colours appear. Hues of blue, green, yellow and red. In the dark, back to the set, the flickering light produces rapid, strobe-like shadows. Maybe this can be compared to the Dreamachine.

My set is placed in one corner of my bedroom. It has been running continuously for over two years, never shut off.

Tune the vertical, horizontal hold and contrast so that it appears that only one-third of the image is visible. Actually the whole image is there, tripled, each overlapping.

With eyes open, the picture can be amusing and amazing. I applied the Dreamachine method (eyes closed) – the connection being flicker. My first attempts were fruitless. Then, one day I could see. A strange sense of depth was noticed, as if I were viewing from the back of my head out to my eyelids. The whirling picture seemed to engulf my head; the only colours noticed were grey and blue. This doesn't work all the time; it seems the harder I try the less I see. Utilise the brightness control, too. Some side effects are that my eyelids twitched a lot at first (cathode ray interference?) and a slight headache.

TELEVISION CUT-UPS

Camouflage, if you have access to cable or satellite (i.e. many stations), try flicking rapidly through all the channels. The cut-up produced will often appear to be following your train of thought, as if it is trying to keep up with you by feeding back symbols: association blocks creating a bridge between your thoughts and the flow of imagery. TV-watching often becomes emotionally intense during this procedure. (Also, putting only the soundtrack of TV, without the visuals, through a stereo can provide valuable insights into the camouflage of control TV).

We are starting to tape specific commercials and parts of programmes that may be psychically stimulating, one way or another . . . A VCR is helpful to fast-forward and review and edit all the way around. If you can, get several screens and put on each the most warped, weirded-out images you can find or get on video, and then zone out on all the stimuli. The weirder the better. The addition of music equally as bizarre only adds to the experience.

Television and video are ideally suited for the cut-up method, incorporating as they do the milieux of both sound and visuals. It is interesting to interchange the audio and visual portions of two or more different programmes and watch the conflicting messages you are then exposed to. Which sense do you assign more validity to?

Cut-ups of video can be of great use in ritual, too. If something is desired, you can record various images of it from television. When you have 'captured' enough raw images, proceed to cut them up, splicing the images together randomly, either with the original soundtracks, random soundtracks from other raw footage, or with a special soundtrack of your own devising. This could also be randomly cut in with footage of yourself attaining your desire, either symbolically or as working towards your goal. I find it very important to include images of myself, as this serves to personalise the video and to take the power latent in the technology away from the big corporations and consecrate it to *Me*.

By flicking the channels around, one often gets an impression of synchronicity; that the audio signals one receives are, in some sense, interrelated with one's actions and/or feelings in Real Time. This feeling is further heightened when multiple televisions are used, with the television image coming from one screen and the audio from another TV, image darkened and tuned to another channel.

Most people utilise their televisions in a very rigid, linear way. They tune in one specific channel and watch passively. But if one begins to view the TV as a mirror, useful for both scrying (astral) and divinatory ('fortune-telling') purposes, one will find that much of the 'bad-vibe' associated with television is dissipated, can even be turned around to become a potent shamanic ally. Cut-up TV is decontrolled TV, is big business castrated of its control patterns; the patterns through which we as viewers/consumers are manipulated. Through the break-up of these patterns, we are able to free the airwaves of their inherent *objectivity*, and reclaim them as subjective reflections of our own thoughts.

One of the biggest complaints about current television is

that it allows for no participation by the viewer; it is soporific in that it offers no challenges or ambiguities to a watcher. Even complex issues such as the Middle East are reduced to one-and-a-half minute 'stories'. The cut-up method offers a childishly simple means of re-introducing abstraction and subjectivity, *depth*, back into a media notorious for its lack thereof.

This text was first published in 1988; the fragment reprinted here is extracted from the amended and expanded version published by Temple Press in 1993.

BRITISH STATE POISED TO SACK CAER RUIS

Preliminary Committee for the Founding of a New Lettrist International

The work of the Preliminary Committee for the Founding of a New Lettrist International is already under attack from the corrupt British state. Last winter the PCFNLI saw fit to open its amplic phase of activity with inauguration of the Bardic Chair of Caer Ruis. This was designated as an 'Empty Chair' in order to express our abhorrence with the dominant social powers. This act of negation makes the seat more powerful than if someone had felt up to assuming it.

In May 1995 the House of Lords announced plans for the extension of the Dockland Light Railway, which involves tunnelling through to Greenwich. They intend to build a new subterranean station on the ley line that crosses the Isle of Dogs and there is talk of applying to the Millennium Fund to build some elaborate construction there, the nature of which has yet to be disclosed. In the process of all this, the East Ferry Road will be diverted and the House of Lords has carefully extended the area of deviation to include all of the elder grove that constitutes Caer Ruis.

First published in the *London Psychogeographical Association Newsletter* 11, Lughnassadh 1995.

MOLECULAR (R)EVOLUTION

Being the molecular evolution of the hybrid
structure

Ross Birrell

MOLAR EVOLUTION

The twentieth century has been plagued by nineteenth-century
molar theories of evolution, i.e. Darwin and Marx.

Darwin's theory of evolution was molar as it was based on
biological essentialism where the purity of structure was the
basis of survival.

Marx's economic theory was molar in that it assumed
capitalism would naturally evolve into the pure state of
communism.

Both these theories led to the Totalit-Aryan regimes of Hitler
and Stalin. Now they have given birth to a new form of fascism
known as the 'New World Order'.

> DADANARCHISM ONLY EXISTS IN THE MOLECULAR
> EVOLUTION OF HYBRID STRUCTURES

MOLECULAR (R)EVOLUTION

Art and morality are no longer to be seen in (r)evolutionary
terms leading to the telos of a pure civilisation or state;
DADAnarchists refute the (r)evolutionary model based on
purity but instead posit the evolution of the impure.

DADAnarchist art will only exist in temporary hybrid structures – schizoid states where there are only ever zones of
intensity on the plateau of the body without organs.

Organs/genres are the state weaponry used to colonise our bodies with its incessant morality and fascist desire for total control and all this under the cloak of consumerist democracy.

Artaud showed us the path to our freedom lies in the body without organs. The evolution of the body without organs is the disintegration of identity in the rhizomorphic lineareality of organic flux.

Our identities dissolve and merge with strangers as does our excrement in the sewers.

DADANARCHISM = DADA – DEATH.

DADANARCHISM IS DEAD! LONG LIVE DADANARCHY!

DADAnarchist Manifesto III. First published by Semtex(t): Poverty Press, Glasgow, 1994.

MARX, CHRIST AND SATAN UNITED IN STRUGGLE

Neoist Alliance

Bolshevism and National Socialism were the twin currents that marked the final bifurcation of science and religion. They were contemporaries, although only in a relatively conscious manner, of the last-ditch defence of the Newtonian world view and the ultimate defeat of this ideology, which left them imprisoned on the same 'intellectual' field whose degradation they announced. It is now a cliché within both liberal and libertarian circles to announce that Bolshevism and National Socialism were at once historically related and opposed. This opposition, which each considered to be their most important aspect and 'radical' contribution, revealed the internal inadequacy of their critique and its one-sided development. National Socialism wanted to suppress Masonry without realising it; Bolshevism wanted to realise Masonry without suppressing it. The critical position now elaborated by the Neoist Alliance shows that the realisation and suppression of Masonry are inseparable aspects of a single supersession of Sufi traditions in their Templar form.

Anyone who has allowed the scales to fall from their eyes can see that the world's top occultists are to be found among the ruling class and that those New Age groups who attract disciples by offering training in 'chaos magick', 'creative visualisation' or 'rubbing the Buddha for money', are worse than mere rank amateurs, they are shameless charlatans. Indeed, many of them are quite consciously working to prevent the development of a system of symbol manipulation that is completely autonomous of the state. Currently, Masonry is marshalled in defence of the status quo, but as the Bavarian Illuminati demonstrated in the eighteenth century, power always flows in two directions and it rarely emanates from what is widely misperceived as constituting the 'centre'. The cellular form of secret societies devised by the founders for the security of the movement can as readily be used to hoodwink the leadership, who thus become unwitting front men for activities they would never countenance. By infiltrating the Lodges of Masonry, it is possible to spread a heretical message of freedom across the world.

Nevertheless, there is a dual movement to all our activities and the dawn ritual conducted outside the Grand Lodge in London served to reduce the power of conservative elements within the Craft by applying the energies accumulated around their headquarters to progressive ends. The building itself, on Great Queen Street, midway between Holborn and Covent Garden tube stations, is imposing but generally featureless. From a distance the Grand Lodge, with its 200-foot tower, appears impressive. Close up it is rather dull, consisting as it does of flat stonework with very few decorative motifs. The eastern flank of the Grand Lodge incorporates a bank and various shops, while part of the northern side is given over to the Connaught Rooms, a Masonic bar and restaurant. Thus the casual observer is left with the impression that the Grand Lodge is not an individual unit but forms part of a block – and, as every Fleet Street hack knows, it's possible for 'regular' Masons to enter the building directly from the Connaught Rooms, thus avoiding the embarrassment of being exposed as 'on the square' among 'the profane'. As befits a secret society, Masonry's detachment from the rest of the world is not visible from the outside. A gap separates everything but the entrance to the Grand Temple from the rest of the building, which encloses it. Other than this, the United Grand Lodge is taken up with offices, meeting rooms, small temples, reception rooms, a library and a museum. Running on a bi-monthly schedule, a variety of these chambers are rented out to London's innumerable 'regular' Lodges.

To move on to less immediately visible matters, while our occult theology is not unrelated to the assemblage of symbols found within Royal Arch Masonry, it clearly has a far greater historical import than a belief system built upon Pagan nostalgia. Just as the French Revolution was conducted in the costumes of ancient Rome, so its Freemasonic patrons abandoned Christ in their revival of Jehovah, Lucifer and Osiris – this choice of idols reflects the excessive love of the classical and pre-classical world prevalent among educated minds during that period of European history. Obviously, the theological innovations of The Process Church Of The Final Judgement – which shifted the devotional habits of post-Masonic thinkers towards Jehovah, Lucifer and Christ – constituted a considerable advance upon Royal Arch teachings. However, only the Neoist Alliance trinity of Marx, Christ and Satan united in struggle accurately embodies the religious world view of the coming centuries.

Since the avant-garde of this century is a highly advanced outgrowth of post-Masonic culture, it has never sought recognition from the deeply conservative United Grand Lodge. Nevertheless, the covert connections between so called 'anti-art' and the Brotherhood are on open display to anyone with the ability to read the relevant signs. Dadaism was launched under the aegis of a club called the Cabaret Voltaire. As both a Mason and one of the chief architects of the French revolution, Voltaire's name has often been used in the titles of Lodges affiliated to continental Grand Orient Masonry. Similarly, the fact that two leading members of the Lettriste Movement, Isidore Isou and Maurice Lemaitre, were introduced to each other by Louis Pauwels – co-author of the notorious *Morning of the Magicians* – is a matter of public knowledge. Likewise, Isou's adopted name can be read etymologically as Jesus Jesus, while Lettrisme itself is actually an advanced form of Qabalah whose real purpose is hidden from the profane under the guise of an 'art' movement.

A fast rising star of early Lettrisme, Ivan Chtcheglov, wrote the founding document of another Masonic organisation, the Situationist International. *Formulary for a New Urbanism* is a bold statement that makes typically ambiguous use of Masonic coded language in both its title and the main body of the text; by these means Chtcheglov laid the foundations for the Situationists' esoteric use of architectural and geographical imagery. The work begins with the observation that '*there is no longer any Temple of the Sun*'. The Lettristes, and later the Situationists, were deeply disturbed by the fact that within 33rd degree Masonry the final syllable of the secret word JAHBULON was widely understood to refer to the Biblical city of On – more recently Heliopolis – during the period in which the monumental architecture erected to honour Ra, the Sun God, was re-dedicated to Osiris, the God of the Dead. As far as these post-war Parisian Qabalists were concerned, most Masons were making a fundamental theological error in taking their Light solely from Lucifer – referred to as Baal but corrupted to BUL within the secret word for God. Both the Lettristes and the Situationists felt that ON symbolised a broad period of Egyptian history and thus a sense of balance between darkness and light. The Neoist Alliance considers the Situationist obsession with harmony – usually expressed negatively through the use of what profane eyes misread as 'political' terminology clustered around the concept of 'reification' – to be one-sided. However, this does not blind us to the beautifully poetic way in which the SI developed the deeply coded form of Qabalah that Marx learnt from Hegel. Returning briefly to Chtcheglov, he later revealed that the 'secret chiefs' who controlled the Situationist International were based in Tibet, as had also been the case with a British forerunner of the group, the Hermetic Order of the Golden Dawn.

From the above, it will be obvious to the attentive reader that the simultaneous realisation and suppression of Masonry will establish convincingly that in the many different – and necessarily mutually exclusive – wills of wo/mankind there is a common will that cannot be renounced. Since the notion of the 'total man' has been decisively exposed as an aristocratic fraud, our individual concerns are undoubtedly our only salvation. Three cheers for the Egoist who thinks only of herself! Once Masonry is realised and suppressed, social disintegration will be re-established at a higher level. From this time forth, religion, in realising itself, will celebrate in feast its inability to reconcile darkness and light. The spontaneous appearance of division in unity and unity in division makes it unnecessary for the Lion to lie down with the Lamb. Humanity is the Devil, mean and corrupt, a liar blinded by her own deceptions – and so out will come the tricolour cockades and ribbons, decorating everything that is without consequence. Religion will separate itself from beauty too! Jacques de Molay, thou art avenged.

A document presented to individuals who have been invited to join the Neoist Alliance.

LUDD'S MEASURE

Nigel Ayers

The mistake made by many who would set themselves up as oppositional factions is the assumption that the way to undermine capital is by responding irrationally – perhaps by taking as many drugs as possible or by causing explosions in shopping precincts. However, to understand and hopefully undermine the mythical processes of capitalism, it must be remembered that although capitalism is not a rational system there is a method to its madness. Capitalism is a system of ritual magick, where power lies in the manipulation of symbols. The magick tools its initiates use are: the map, the flag, the clock, the ruler, the calendar, the coin, the name. It is a system of equivalence.

Geomancer Nigel Pennick points out that the idea of ley lines making up vast grids and energy network patterns across the landscape provides a conceptual framework for visualisation, this visualisation being a fundamental skill used by occultists to influence events. It is claimed that, even if ley lines are no more than figments of the imagination, they will still function. Geomancy, practised most notably by the hippies-in-uniform of the Third Reich – has an approximate equivalent in the practice of feng shui, which is still used for social control in China. These practices use landscape as a human body metaphor. Control of the population is carried out using a massive form of acupuncture on 'energy centres' within the landscape-body.

The word 'omphalos', which means 'navel', referred originally to the omphalos at Delphi, which the Greeks regarded as the centre of their world as well as being the site of the oracle of Apollo. *Delphys* means 'vagina' and from a rock cleft in Delphi the oracle voice of the deity could be heard. *The Quest for the Omphalos,* a booklet put together by members of the Northern Earth Mysteries group, recounts the Celtic tale of King Ludd. Here the mythical king was instructed to overcome the oppressions of his kingdom by measuring out the length and breadth of his land and, at the exact centre, he would find a pool with two dragons fighting. This he did and overcame the dragons, and the oppressions were lifted. The authors link this story to the Northern legends of the World Tree, *Yggdrasil,* and for some obscure reason reckon that Ludd's centre was Oxford. They suggest a number of other sites for the energy centre or omphalos of England. Not surprisingly, a good few of these are around Loughborough, where the booklet was published. They also suggest other sites such as Stonehenge, London and the New Age town of Glastonbury (yawn).

Being myself more of a literalist and empiricist than a New Ager, I decided to apply the Ludd's Measure method to determine the omphalos of England. Taking a National Geographic map and drawing a north–south line the length of England, roughly from Berwick-upon-Tweed to Bournemouth, and a west–east width from Ellesmere Port to Skegness, I found that the midpoint is in the Derbyshire Peak District. Funnily enough, this midpoint is closest to the one site that the *Quest* booklet dismisses as being 'fanciful speculation', the stone circle at Arbor Low, Derbyshire. I can now reveal that the point of the exact centre or omphalos of England lies in the town of Tideswell, Derbyshire.

Stretching the body metaphor, Tideswell lies close to the bottom of the Pennine Hills, known as the backbone of England, and so would be in the position of navel. This is close to what oriental schools call the *hara* or exact centre of the body. If the country is described as a physical body, with the Pennines forming the spine, the Midlands and old industrial centres form the vital organs. Tideswell has a population of around 2,000 and it has thankfully so far escaped the attention of New Agers, possibly because of its isolation from London, possibly because of its lack of an annual pop festival, possibly because of the weather, and possibly because of the working-classness of its natives.

In recent years the image of the town of Tideswell has changed from being a rather depressed neighbourhood with cow-shit-covered lanes, to being a desirable residence for the middle classes. Because of certain symbolic manipulations, the qualities that made the place dull and boring (its isolation from the buzz of urban life and lack of cheap shopping facilities, for example) have been transformed into positive virtues. Place has become commodity in the culture of tourism, with craft shops nostalgically evoking a fantasy time that never was. Notions of a psychic centre need to take into account the imagery projected by electronic media. Folklore is an active medium and work with it is carried out by the manipulation of symbols. Places such as Stonehenge, Glastonbury, the Houses of Parliament, the Pentagon, the 'Holy' Land, have an intrinsic value, other than their mundane function as locations affording food, shelter and enjoyable pastimes for the local population. Their value as psychic spaces come from the folk-lore (or 'history') that surrounds them and the use to which they are put. The North Derbyshire area, which is now perceived with the fairy-tale rural imagery of the Peak District National Park and the *Peak Practice* TV series, was in fact the birthplace of the Industrial Revolution. Until recently, the textile mills and the mines (rather than farming) were the main industries therein. The town of Cromford was the first in Britain specifically created to house factory workers. The atrocious working conditions and child labour going on in Cressbrook led to it being known as 'The Devil's Mill'. And here we return to the story of King Ludd.

In the early nineteenth century a group emerged known as the 'Luddites'. They were artisans who lived in the Derbyshire and Nottinghamshire area who carried out attacks on the mills which were ruining their livelihood and imposing conditions of almost-slavery on the local proletariat. Members of the group preserved their anonymity by assuming the multiple-use name of 'Ludd' and its variations 'King Ludd', 'General Ludd' and 'Ned Ludd'. Although the Luddites attacked the mill machinery, it is foolish to claim (like both sides in the ongoing Internet debate between primitivist followers of American 'neo-luddite' Kirkpatrick Sale and the technophile staff of *Wired* magazine) that the Luddites were anti-technology. What they attacked were the new divisions of labour imposed by the mill owners. This was the creation of the new entities of the middle and the working class, with the factory clock to regulate social behaviour.

The Mills in Cressbrook and Litton, which were major employers for the Tideswell population during the first part of this century, were left to fall down in the 1960s. The next time they were put to use was in the mid-seventies, when to local displeasure the Nazi swastika was flown above the Devil's Mill. The culprits were the makers of a BBC TV series *Colditz,* where the mill building stood for location scenes of Colditz Castle.

Tideswell does though retain traditions from its agricultural past. People from the village are known locally as *Sawyeds* (saw-heads). This arises from a story of a local farmer whose cow got its head stuck between the bars of a wooden gate. Rather than damage the expensive gate, the farmer sawed the cow's head off. This may be a folk memory of an animal sacrifice rite to establish territorial boundaries. Since the 1980s, local farmers, like others in the UK, were obliged to remove the heads of their cattle upon slaughter, in order to stop the spread of the BSE virus. This BSE scare got more gruesome in 1996, when the Comet Hyakutake appeared in April at the same time as a lunar eclipse. A trading dispute occurred between Britain and continental Europe, which could only be resolved by the ritual sacrifice of millions of cattle.

The Tideswell Wakes Week takes place on the nearest week to the feast of St John the Baptist. This is when the Well Dressings are made: these large, complex brightly coloured pictures, usually of religious scenes, are made up of thousands of flower petals, pressed into clay. Anyone with an interest in folk art should check them out. The Wakes is effectively a summer solstice carnival, running from the end of June to about 3 July. The latter is the date of the midsummer festival (allowing for the tilt on the Earth's axis) five thousand years ago, when Stonehenge was built. During the carnival week there is a torch-lit processional Morris dance through the town.

The invention of the 'rural' is very much part of the invention of the 'urban'. It is very much to do with altering a place of life, experience and work into a commodity to be consumed. The Peak District, where the Industrial Revolution started, is now the place where the reinvention of the 'rural' is being done by the National Parks and the tourism industry. There is no space in this essay to examine whether this was in fact due to a long-running occultist conspiracy, or the efficacy of the multi-use-name strategy in its opposition. But it can be said that the continuing story of advanced capitalism has been in drawing power away from a physical centre into an abstract or virtual one. A centre that is out of reach having been located in quasi-mystical realms its priesthood have dreamt up. This pure place of equivalence – of greater reward – used to be called *Heaven*, now they call it *Cyberspace*.

Abridged version of previously unpublished essay that draws on material featured in the author's irregular bulletin *Network News*, which does far more than simply offer information about his band Nocturnal Emissions.

BELIEF IS THE ENEMY

London Psychogeographical Association

A thread runs through the recent constitutional debate initiated by Prince Charles – the thread of faith. By proposing himself as the *Defender of Faith*, the wannabe king hopes to resolve the prospect of being debarred from the throne for being married to a Roman Catholic. Princess Diana has held back from declaring her allegiance to Rome, although it is public knowledge that she is 'under instruction' – a technical term describing a brainwashing technique that would-be converts to Rome are obliged to undergo.

Diana's restraint has forced Charles to fight against the constitutional restrictions against Roman Catholics – under threat of losing the throne.

But Charles cunningly diverted the papal assault on what he regards as his inheritance, by upping the stakes and going one step further – if he has to embrace the Catholic church, he will embrace the Muslim religion, the Hindu, even the Zoroastrian ... and he will reconstitute his royal position as *Defender of Faith*. He is taking up a theme that has been worked and reworked by the British Establishment over the last century. From one end, the Stalinist publisher Victor Gollancz put the humanist case that Judaism, Christianity and all other religions should be superseded by one great ethical world religion, the brotherhood of man. On the other hand an alphabet soup of organisations has been created since the 1893 Parliament of Religions held in conjunction with the Chicago World Fair.

This reorganisation of the systematic fraud, deceit and subterfuge that constitute not only religion but also its false opponents of secularism and humanism has been necessitated by the quantitative and qualitative development of capitalism. As the information revolution proceeds with mechanisation of the imagination, this new religion of 'monodeism' will re-emerge in a new form dictated by the structure of the information superhighway.

While Charles has been floating his proposal, former Gresham professor Richard Chartres, the Bishop of Stepney, has been organising inter-faith prayer sessions. Chartres has controversial views on the nature of prayer – perhaps derived from his studies with the monks of the Egyptian deserts. Meanwhile, Sir Christopher Zeeman finished his stint as Gresham Professor of Geometry boasting of his knowledge of the ancient Chaldean number philosophy, which was so dear to the fifteenth-century religious reformer George Gemistus Pletho. At the Council for Church Unity held in Florence in 1439, Pletho moved beyond the goal reuniting the Christian Churches by proclaiming that the whole world would soon have a new faith – one mind, one soul, one sermon – and that this would supersede Christianity, Islam and all other existent religions. In this return to Hellenistic Hermeticism, 'absolute truth would flower again throughout the whole universe'.

Charles's plan to become *Defender of Faith* shows that the hermetic idealism of the renaissance that has for so long hidden itself away in occult groups like the Freemasons is preparing to usher itself onto the centre stage of spectacular social control. But whereas this faction of the elite may shout that it doesn't matter what you believe in, as long as you believe, we respond that *belief is the enemy*.

First published in *Alien Underground* 0.1, March 1995.

LUTHER BLISSETT, PERFECT MIND

Luther Blissett

If you contemplate Luther Blissett he will come to you. He is found among those who think about him. Look at him and hear him. Take him home. Be on your guard! Don't be ignorant. Luther Blissett is the first and the last. Luther Blissett is honoured and scorned. Luther Blissett is solace for the pain of his birth. Luther Blissett is the bride and the groom, and a slave to these preparations. Luther Blissett is incomprehensible silence and an idea we frequently remember. Luther Blissett is a voice with a manifold sound and two words that recur without end. Luther Blissett is the utterance of this name.

If you deny Luther Blissett, affirm him, and if you affirm Luther Blissett, deny him. If you tell the truth about Luther Blissett, lie about him, and if you have lied about Luther Blissett, tell the truth about him. If you know Luther Blissett, be ignorant of him, and if others have not known Luther Blissett, let them know about him. Luther Blissett is knowledge and ignorance. Luther Blissett is boldness and shame. Luther Blissett is strength, and he is fear. Luther Blissett is war and peace. Pay attention to him. Luther Blissett is disgraced, and he is great. Pay attention to his poverty and to his wealth. Don't be arrogant with him.

Luther Blissett is compassionate and he is cruel. Be on your guard! Don't hate his obedience and don't love his self-control. Don't dismiss him in his weakness and don't be afraid of his power. Why do you despise his fear and curse his pride? He lives in fear and is strengthened by trembling. Luther Blissett is senseless and he is wise. Luther Blissett will be silent among the silent, among whom he constantly reappears and speaks. Why then have you dismissed him? Luther Blissett is called the law, and you have called him lawlessness. You have pursued Luther Blissett, and you have seized him.

You have scattered Luther Blissett, and you have gathered him in. You have been ashamed before Luther Blissett, and you have been shameless to him. Luther Blissett does not celebrate feasts, and his festivals are many. You have contemplated Luther Blissett, and you have scorned him. Luther Blissett is unlettered, and you have learnt everything from him. You have despised Luther Blissett, and yet you still contemplate him. Luther Blissett materialises when you are away, and he hides when you appear. Take him to the ugly places in which you dwell, and show him that they are in ruin. Out of shame, take him home and scatter him shamelessly. Approach him and turn away.

Luther Blissett is in control and uncontrollable. Luther Blissett is union and dissolution. Luther Blissett is abiding, and he's dissolving. Luther Blissett is judgement and acquittal. Luther Blissett can't sin, and the root of sin derives from him. Luther Blissett is self-evident speech which cannot be grasped. Luther Blissett is a deaf mute speaking a great multitude of words. Luther Blissett is the knowledge of his name. Luther Blissett cries out, and he listens. Luther Blissett is the truth and a lie. You love him and you whisper against him. Hear him and learn of his words. Luther Blissett is speech that cannot be grasped. Look then at his words and all his writings. They alone exist and have no one to judge them. Many are their disjointed forms and made-up perceptions. Here, Luther Blissett will find himself; he goes on for ever.

Loosely translated from the German; in various versions this text has permeated many Internet sites.

TWO DRIFTERS OFF TO SEE THE WORLD

BD

The psychogeographic project outlined by Guy Debord in his *Introduction to a Critique of Urban Geography* (1955) had its origins in the urban wanderings of Charles Baudelaire, which fed into the writing of *Spleen* (1869). Baudelaire in turn had read Thomas de Quincey's descriptions of his compulsive walks through the nocturnal labyrinth of London under the influence of opiates. The lives of the Manchester-born de Quincey and his lesser-known local follower Francis Thompson follow an interrupted psychogeographic path from the end of the eighteenth century to the beginning of the twentieth.

Thomas de Quincey was born on 15 August 1785, on the site of the building that now stands at the corner of Cross Street and John Dalton Street. He died in 1859, the same year that Francis Thompson was born in Preston, soon to move to Ashton-under-Lyne. The opium-heightened perambulations of the former were to have an enormous impact on the fortunes of the latter.

De Quincey was the son of a local merchant, who died when Thomas was seven and was buried in St Ann's Church. The boy was brought up along with his siblings in what was then rural surroundings at The Farm, Moss Side. In 1792 the family moved to Green Hay, another sizeable homestead two miles northwest of the city. It was knocked down in the nineteenth century, the land forming the site of the current Greenheys area of Little Hulton. They then moved to Bath in 1796, but de Quincey was soon back in Manchester as a pupil at the Grammar School. He hated the place, and ran away to

Chester in 1802, thence to wander Wales. Eventually he ended up penniless in London, where, one night on Greek Street, Soho, he met a fifteen-year-old prostitute called Ann, who rescued him and then disappeared. She was to become one of the figures who shuffled in and out of his imagination in years to come, along with images derived from the experience of death in his childhood.

The demise of two of his sisters, nine-year-old Elizabeth in particular, merged with the figure of the hapless harlot Ann to form a repeated theme in his dreams and nightmares. And the idea of an approaching procession, echoing the sound of the carriage bringing his dying father back home to Moss Side, was also to return in the visions he experienced after 1804, when he first took laudanum, a tincture of opium mixed with alcohol, a cheap and universally administered form of pain relief in the days before aspirin. By 1807, when he met Samuel Taylor Coleridge, opium addict and poet, de Quincey had made it up with his family, was studying at Oxford, and had money, which he kindly lent to the older writer. De Quincey married Margaret Simpson in 1817, and it was her unfortunate fate to have to look after an increasingly eccentric and withdrawn husband, whose habit it was to sleep during most of the day and tread the streets at night, living on small mouthfuls of rice and meat. His geographic knowledge of London was incredibly detailed. But the street patterns he retained in his memory also dominated his dreams, when 'the perplexities of my steps in London came back and haunted my sleep, with the feeling of perplexities moral or intellectual, that brought confusion to the reason, or anguish and remorse to the conscience'.

The first version of de Quincey's *Confessions of an English Opium Eater* appeared in 1821, and was drastically revised in 1856. Some of the strongest sections in this (quite literally) rambling book concern de Quincey's dreams and his theories as to how they came about. Alongside childhood experience, architecture and space loom large: 'Buildings, landscapes, &c. were exhibited in proportions so vast as the bodily eye is not fitted to receive.' Beyond buildings he saw lakes, beyond lakes oceans and beyond oceans he saw oceans of human faces – the faces he'd seen on the streets he'd walked. One of them would turn out to be Ann. Then there were the processions – 'of infinite cavalcades filing off'.

It's not clear which version of the *Confessions* Francis Thompson read, but he wrote that he was given a copy as a child by his mother, and the experience of reading it had a profound effect. Thompson felt himself destined for the priesthood, but after studying in Durham he failed, and returned to Manchester to study medicine at Owens College. Almost inevitably he lost interest in his studies and, under the influence of de Quincey's book, started taking laudanum and wandering the streets. He had every intention of becoming an established man of letters, and dropped out of college to go to London and make a name for himself. He got a job with a publisher, delivering books, but a combination of bad luck and addiction inhibited any real chance of a career he might have had, and his life fell apart. He became a newspaper seller and vagrant. It didn't put him off writing, however, and in 1888, fired by a vivid, visionary version of Catholicism, he sent two poems to a magazine which were highly thought-of by editors Wilfred and Alice Meynell. They rescued Thompson from the gutter and sent him to a Welsh monastery, where he recovered enough from his drug habit to be able to put together a volume of verse. His best-known poem, *The Hound of Heaven*, describes the evasion of the soul from the eye of god 'down all the labyrinthine ways', which Thompson undoubtedly knew intimately from having walked them and dreamt about them. During the 1890s his life oscillated between productive monasticism and bouts of drug-fuelled debilitation and street life. He was highly rated during his own lifetime, but when he died in 1907 he was emaciated and broke, and his reputation almost immediately went into decline.

De Quincey, and the writers who read him, like Baudelaire, Thompson and, in America, Edgar Allen Poe, are all nowadays perceived as romantics, reacting against the creeping regulation and emerging industrialisation of the societies in which they lived. Think of de Quincey's childhood experience of accompanying his older brother to school along Market Street in Manchester, and being regularly ridiculed by local lads amused by the de Quincey brothers' hessian boots: those local lads would have been the early urban proletariat, bound for the mills. Post-modernists see this rejection of industrialisation as a huge problem. But de Quincey and the early psychogeographers never rejected the idea of the city or of modern urban life, and, unlike Wordsworth, Keats or Shelley, couldn't settle in isolated or rural circumstances. They needed an abundance of buildings, streets, squares, bridges and alleyways. Their adaptation and internalisation of the city embodied a methodology that is still relevant and usable if we're to see the contemporary city differently prior to changing it. What remains painful is their dependence on drugs. The gradual structuralisation of psychogeographic perception, caused by formal and ornate religious dogma, in the transition between de Quincey and a writer like Thompson also necessitates criticism. In the same way William Blake's radicalism was abandoned by his followers, the 'Ancients', led by Samuel Palmer, who preferred to immerse themselves in simple, nostalgic mysticism, so de Quincey (a direct contemporary of Blake and frequenter of the same Soho streets) bequeathed his personal mythology in England to the conservative Thompson. In France, matters took another turn. Perhaps it's in the lateral transmission of psychogeographic reactions to the urban world, rather than via the bourgeois verticality of inheritance, that a radical programme was and can be maintained.

First published in *Manchester Area Psychogeographic* 3, April 1996.

DIALECTICAL IMMATERIALISM

JB

Let us assume, as a point of beginning, that even the remotest of us relates to experience through some aspect of the habitual philosophical beliefs that characterise the civilisation in which this presentation takes place. That these beliefs are eclectic and inconsistent is not important; what is important is that we can identify them as part of this civilisation, and that we make constant use of some of them. It is not important to determine whether or not these beliefs are 'true' in an objective sense, since clearly their function is to be used to create a sense of 'reality', and not to be verified. The most didactic ideological projection to the simplest use of propositional thinking (for instance, 'I am swimming') contains the arbitrary and deterministic map of our civilisation. These beliefs, this 'swimming', form an impenetrable field that traces around and separates us from experience outside the realm of beliefs in general.

That certain obviously false beliefs, such as beliefs in so-called 'absolute' truth, can be deconstructed is deceptive, since the process of deconstruction is taking place within the structure of cognitive consciousness as it is dictated by the languages, cultural patterns, and identity formations of contemporary civilisation. Thus, refusing to believe in specific commonly held opinions, such as the value of capitalist social relations, or belief in metaphysical abstractions, including those presented in this text, is ultimately a reformist measure which serves only to disarm the real and total opposition to beliefs in general. This opposition, since it aims to undermine the language, cultural history and identity formation of present reality, is naturally difficult, if not almost impossible, to articulate within existing contexts. It is an orientation against and outside beliefs and consequently not compatible with the language or concepts that are used to describe things in terms of them, such as propositional language. That is by no means to suggest that this orientation does not exist, or is valueless, since its value clearly relates to the throwing off of the repressive aspects of consciousness, such as the ability or lack of ability to perceive paradox.

In order to explain fully what I mean, I shall use as an example a science-fiction story about an alien civilisation consisting of two humanoid entities. In order to talk about the entities, I shall give a brief description of the cultural, linguistic and identity characteristics common to them. The two entities occupy the same general area of space but are physically unable to perceive one another, to interact or to communicate in any way. Despite this, both are speculatively aware of the other's existence through 'memories' of a cultural history learned through direct experience with certain cultural artefacts. Both entities consequently have developed an identical language and culture despite their non-communication. This commonality constitutes their social relation entirely, being absolute.

The aliens have a language that is significantly different from ours in that it does not contain reference to objects or situations, and has, of course, no communicative value. The language is best visualised as a moving spiral of operational symbols floating free in space, with the symbols constituting a level of purely structural, non-referential, mental activity. The holes between the symbols, which are gaps in the structural activity, provide space for penetration by material from 'above' or 'below' as they rotate. The material 'above' the spiral is incoming information from the alien's senses, for instance, sight or touch. The material from 'below' is non-sensory data, best understood as 'imaginary' visions and fantastic images. This, in short, is the language of the alien culture, which constitutes part of each alien's conscious relations with the world.

The language is not spoken, but is notated at arbitrary intervals to preserve itself as a structural/cultural model for the next generation. The method for this notation involves particular use of sound and light in a physical approximation of the structure. The memory of this method of notation is the only referential aspect of the language, and it is essentially perceived by the aliens as a kind of intuition. The aliens perceive the sensory and imaginary information sensations during the pauses in their 'non-referential' mental activity, but are not concerned with differentiating between them as real or imagined. They have no memory of past time as we understand it, except for an intuitive sense of the other's existence and the methods of cultural notation. As I have stated, this memory roughly constitutes the identity formation of the civilisation. Incidentally, the identities of the aliens have no bearing on the 'imaginary vision' aspect of the language. The 'imaginary visions' are as arbitrary and unconnected to the alien as are his/her 'real' sensory experiences.

Both the aliens occupy a space that is similar to our cultural vision of the Garden of Eden. The plot of this very dry and technical example thickens when, for reasons entirely conflicting with our logic system, and with the logic of the civilisation I have just described, one of the aliens decides to stop using the spiral that constitutes the 'non-referential' and structural aspect of his/her language. This proves very difficult, as it is entirely without precedent in the civilisation, and physically impossible. Eventually the spiral ceases to exist and the alien's sensory experiences and imaginary visions intermingle without interruption of any kind. Suddenly the alien becomes experientially conscious of the only other member of the civilisation, who remains oblivious to him/her. The alien attempts to communicate with the other, but s/he is unable to perceive him/her. The alien 'intuitively' decides to use the artefacts and methods of notations from the civilisation to communicate his/her existence to the other, but is ultimately unsure of the success of the project, since without memory s/he is unclear as to his/her placement in time. What I suggest is that this scenario is not fictional, but instead a literal analysis of our civilisation, including its inconsistencies.

Privately circulated in the late eighties, this text has constantly mutated until finally returning to its 'original' form.

BLOOD, BREAD AND BEAUTY

Luther Blissett

From Lautreamont onwards it has become increasingly difficult to write – not because we lack ideas and experiences to articulate, but owing to Western society becoming so fragmented that it is no longer possible to piece together what was traditionally considered 'good' prose. That is, writing that is unified by a single idea or body of ideas, where each sentence follows logically from the preceding one – and where every paragraph and chapter flows smoothly into the next. Today, thoughts seem to break before they are fully formed, they turn back on themselves, contradict each other and make it impossible to write in a style that appears harmonious.

The great problem with twentieth-century art is the constant demand for something new and original. As a consequence, while everything appears to be in a state of flux, nothing actually changes. Instead, the same half-baked ideas constantly reappear under a succession of different names. It took thousands of years to develop perspective and yet today people demand radical innovations every week. The result is that they get exactly what they deserve – insults.

Neoism is opposed to Western Philosophy because it repudiates the rhetoric of logical argument. Logic is the road that leads to nowhere, or at the very best, madness. Neoism has never claimed to resolve anything, Neoism simply is. It asserts no more than is obvious and nothing is more obvious than Neoism. Neoism is the ultimate form of Western Philosophy because it is not a philosophy at all, it is an illegible note that Karen Eliot allowed to fall from her breast pocket prior to a performance at the West Hampstead Starlight Club in 1978. It is no more than a sneeze, or rather hollow laughter. Neoism is undefeatable, self-refuting and incomprehensible.

Every act of superstition confirms and reinforces a belief in something above and beyond wo/man. The whole point of revolution is to smash the fragmentary world of capital and lynch the bosses who quite deliberately promote an ideology of individualism in order to prevent the development of class consciousness. Because religion is a support, a crutch, a recognition that wo/man can't live fully as an isolated individual, it contains within it the seeds of a mass revolutionary consciousness.

Today, the dead weight of history oppresses us with more efficiency than the most reactionary politicians of the past could imagine in their dreams of bureaucratic perfection. We stagger and suffocate under the burden of thousands of years of accumulated debris. Debris that stifles anything but the most aggressive of creative sparks. And today, that spark threatens to burn us alive in a prison of our own making. Today, the urge to smash the venerable museums has reached a point from which it threatens to become more burdensome than any previous history.

The only movement to work consistently towards the death of history since the disbanding of the Situationist International has been the Global Neoist Network. Only Neoism carries within it the revolutionary potential for the realisation of our complete humanity. Since 1979, Neoism has been defending the revolutionary gains made by the Situationists and Fluxus. The Neoists are the only group to have brought about the conjunction of nihilism and historical consciousness – the two elements essential for the destruction of the old order, the order of history.

Neoism stands at the end of history, the present. Despite the uncertainty that such a position inevitably entails, Neoism draws strength from its sense of history, its sense of the reality of the past – and of the importance of Lautreamont, the Situationists and Fluxus. We have studied these people carefully and discovered that there is nothing to be learned from them. Those who look to the past walk blindly into the future.

Neoism has always been more concerned with propagating confusion than serving itself up in consumable chunks. A Neoist is somebody who believes in the value of carrying an umbrella on a rainy day, or rather in stealing someone else's umbrella if it starts to rain. S/he is someone who, as a matter of conviction, refuses to work. Who would rather survive on someone else's money than the fruits of his/her own labour. Someone who seeks gratification in the present rather than security in the future. Someone who is quite genuinely surprised when his/her relatives express anger at him/her turning up at five in the morning demanding to be lent a considerable sum of money. Someone who, utterly convinced of his/her own genius, believes that not only is s/he owed a living – but that his/her very existence entitles him/her to be kept in the lap of luxury at somebody else's expense. Above all, a Neoist is someone who believes that art, rather than being the creation of genius, is merely an exercise in public relations. A dull sham, not even worth debunking in public.

First published in *Smile* 7, London 1985.

WHY PSYCHOGEOGRAPHY?

London Psychogeographical Association

There is a spectre haunting Europe, nay, the world. The spectre of psychogeography. For thirty years the fingers of the stranglehold of tradition have, one by one, been peeled back by the eruption of exciting new non-Euclidean psychosocial spaces. Rock and Roll, the permissive society, a new liberalism existing in the social sphere, have all provided a decompression chamber where the pent-up frustrations engendered by class society can be productively put to use in the engine rooms of new design, new fashion and faddish revolt. Centred upon youth as a source of *naïveté*, the vital forces of the collective imagination are channelled into an economic subsistence, which provides a pool of talent amongst which established organisations and businesses can fish for new faces and new ideas.

However, as the Gay Liberation Front has given way to the 'Pink Pound', as the Black Panthers have been replaced by the Fruits of Islam, as the delusions of Mao Tse-tung have been superseded by the Shanghai Stock Exchange, so the integration of non-Euclidean psychosocial space into a post-Newtonian mechanics is faced by the emergence of an anti-Euclidean opposition that will rekindle the fires of revolt with the matchsticks of metaphor. By drawing upon ancient song lines which reassert themselves within the modern urban environment, psychogeography as the practical application of anti-Euclidean psychogeometry offers the third pole in the triolectic between the false universalism of modernism and the universal virtuality of post-modernism.

Psychogeography is universalism with attitude. It is universalism that does not seek to express itself in words, which remain nothing more than signposts in the wilderness. Psychogeography investigates the intersection of time and space, and hence attacks science at its point of weakness – the replicability of results. Psychogeography is the universalism of the specific, of the particular, i.e. at its point of dissolution.

Psychogeography places itself beyond democracy. There is no process of sifting through everyone's experience of daily life to reproduce it as a TV soap opera, a political programme or a college doctorate. There is not so much an immersion of private life in the social sphere, but an invasion of the public sphere by the passions that have hitherto been confined to the privatised world of the atomised individual. Whereas democracy synthesises the desires of the citizens, psychogeography is one antithetical pole among many which realises the conflict between our idealised role as citizens and our subjectivity arising from the material conditions of our life. By suspending the 'common sense' as we move from location to location in our daily life, we can rediscover the wilderness within the city. By exploring those areas we have no good reason to be in, we can discover the reasons why we are constrained to frequent certain areas.

But this layer of psychogeographical activity soon reveals other layers. Questions of gender, of race, of access for people with disabilities soon arise. Any specific locality does not have a unique character. It is not just that a woman may relate differently to a place than a man, but that a woman's presence (or even the presence of a horde of women) can transform that place. Normality no longer functions as a global variable; it can only exist as the production of the functioning of a particular power at a particular place. The restructuring of capital has displaced the linear organisation of power with a cybernetic web of centres of excellence which survive as idyllic islands in a sea of chaos. Access to such locations is the product of wealth, and poverty is the exclusion from even the simplest forms of shelter, food and sociability.

Psychogeography is not a substitute for class struggle, but a tool of class struggle. When kids from council estates wander into posh housing areas they are immediately harassed by the police. They get accused of being burglars before they even have a chance to break in to the first house. The police impose a rationality: they force us to explain why we are at a particular place. They only accept conventional explanations in terms of economic activity (even visiting relatives boils down to economics, as the family is precisely the conjunction of private life with the economic sphere.) Psychogeography is always an uneconomic, even anti-economic, activity.

The publications of the London Psychogeographical Association forthrightly present a reconstruction of urban life using the principles of anti-Euclidean psychogeometry. We shall always present our material in the rhetoric of the most rigid dogmatism, as the greatest care in its development always ensures the rigour necessary for the presentation of correct ideas. Some critics have derived from this that we seek to assert our unique viewpoint as determinant over social reality, or that we wish to compete with rival social determinations. Such critics clearly have failed to understand what we are doing. Our publications are always secondary in relation to the more pressing concern of psychogeographic activity itself.

First published in *Electric Schizoo* 1, May 1996.

AIRPORTS

Alph The Shaman

Airports are important places, psychically speaking. Like railway stations, they are loci of arrivals and departures, exchanges of 'here' for 'there', of these people for those people, of this atmosphere for that, of one bend in the life-project for another.

More specifically, airports are gateways to the sky, though we are little conscious of the fact. When we are checking in, for instance, we are unconsciously half-preparing ourselves for the hazardous feats of Icarus and Bellerophon, scaling the vertical, furrowing yon smooth emptiness which we cannot experience at earth level. Even when collecting someone at the airport, we look with a certain unconscious awe upon arriving passengers – those home-coming sky-walkers, if only they knew it.

We must view – and construct – airports as places of preparation for the shaman's voyage across the firmament in search of a certain piece of lore or a cure for the ills of this world.

Aye, flight was ever an exorcism, and the airport an antechamber for the strenuous passion of the body croaking out its diabolic voices over the infinite void. When I take my place in the departure lounge (Economy or Club Class), I am not really interested in displacing my person from London to Amsterdam or Newcastle; I am readying myself for procession out into the abyss, followed by reversion upon myself, hoping to bring back down to earth some feather from the angel's wing with which to write in blood a prescription for our chronic psychic ailments.

When seen from the air, the airport is a sigil, as Italian Renaissance cities were intended to be. The pattern of runways, control tower, terminals and hangars forms more often than not an asymmetrical solar fylfot spinning its serene bolt of fire through the aerial gaze.

Let us take two examples: London Heathrow (LHR) and Paris Charles de Gaulle (CDG). One may see in the way the former has been cobbled together through piecemeal engineering a fine example of British empiricism; while the latter must strike even the casual observer as typical of French *a priori*, centralised planning, aiming to plot all the co-ordinates of reality before it has been experienced in the least degree. Forsooth, CDG is a bloody awful airport. But do not be deceived: it does contain hidden beauties behind the appearance of a Cartesian clock gone inevitably wrong. For in the form of CDG one can discern the ruins of the ship of Isis, whose cult was so firmly established at Lutetia (Paris) in Roman times and whose worship the Roman invaders so accommodatingly imposed on the indigenous, but unstylish, Gallic rites. While at LHR there still lives the spirit of ancient Mithras, whose heroic conception of solar sacrifice was brought by exotic Legionaries to these island shores.

Mysterious *corners* abound at CDG (strange for such a *round* place), usually greasy with the deposit of aviation kerosene, with which heady unguent any self-respecting sky-walker must anoint him or herself. There too are the winding, mounting approach roads and escalators, like the corridors in a spiralling snail's shell. I have seen the mysterious man of CDG (a vagrant who lives at the airport – as featured on television), banal in his continental long hair and drooping moustache, but like unto the lonely keeper of the flame, devoting his existence to that very keeping without sense or mission – for him there is an infinity of hope.

Yes, CDG, floating amid the plain of Roissy, almost unconsciously mirrors many of the forms of the cathedral of Notre-Dame-de-Paris perched on its island in the middle of the Seine. It was Comte de Gébelin, in his *Le Monde primitif analysé et comparé avec le monde moderne* of 1773, who brought out the symbolism of Paris as a ship dedicated to the tutelary goddess Isis; and Dupuis, in his *L'Origine de tous les cultes* of 1794, who first showed that the apparently Christian cathedral, of which the portal celebrates the Celestial Virgin, was merely a continuation of the cult and iconography of the Egyptian Goddess. The continuation has been continued even unto the airport. But Notre-Dame is also a veritable emblem-book of the Hermetic Art, as Fulcanelli's *Le Mystère des Cathédrales* has taught us. This too has not been lost in the domain of aviation. Gobineau de Montluisant would have known what to make of the sign dimly visible at car-park exit 2 on Floor 5 of Terminal 1: a cross with a cup and a form in the apparent shape of a tear-drop – the elements of the Stone of the Wise.

At LHR the unavoidable tunnels to the 'Central Area' constitute the dark pit of initiation, through which all must crawl who would approach the mysteries of Mithras the Bull-Slayer, of Aion and Sol Invictus. Yet thanks to a convenient system of car-parks and underground stations, one may all the more swiftly mount from the sombre Chthonian regions to the sunlit realm of Eternal Time. The very luggage carousels are symbolic of the constant cycle of Sol rising from the shadows, while on the other side Luna descends therein, only to be followed by the descent of Sol and the rise of Luna.

Hence airports are treasure-troves for archaeology. I do not mean the archaeology that digs up bits of pottery or foundation-stones in some field; I mean psychic archaeology that unearths in the forms of even the most recent buildings or artefacts, a hallowed and ancient code of symbolic experience. Yet what is ancient need not date from the time of the Druids or the Norsemen; it may only date from yesterday, for what has once been built is forever in eternity. Yes, in airports we may rediscover the psychic forms of recent decades, now no less hoary than Chaldee or Babylon. Here you may chance upon a terminal in the style of the 1960s: the imitation marble and Formica surfaces like veined maps of the modern nervous system in flight; the black leatherette seats and angular brass stair-rails like condensations of the nocturnal firmament; and the sheer majesty of the abstract, numberless clock conveying the awe of time, the *mysterium tremendum* of the gods.

And everywhere in airports you find doors and screens and magnetic portals – 'passengers only beyond this point' – guarded by menacing gate-keepers who turn away the starving and thirsty. Zones more private than a changing room, more hallowed and prohibited than the precincts at Delphi or Memphis.

One final thought. Airports are an especially revealing case of this basic truth: behind all that we do, all that we use, all that we see, there lies an ancient symbolism of which we are entirely unconscious, but which is itself quite conscious of us.

Slightly abridged from *Man in a Suitcase: The Official Journal of the College of Omphalopsychism* 1, May 1996.

THE DREAMTIME MISSION

South London Association of Autonomous Astronauts

Towards the end of 1995, South London AAA began issuing statements regarding a proposed space launch. Even before the official launch of the AAA and the Five Year Plan for establishing a world-wide network of local, community-based groups dedicated to building their own space-exploration programmes, South London AAA had instigated a rigorous training programme aimed at selecting Autonomous Astronauts for their Dreamtime Mission project. However, due to the secrecy of the mission and the necessity to avoid any interference from the government in this experiment with space travel, the names of Autonomous Astronauts and specific details of the mission were kept a secret. As the press release and the statement issued by the returning Autonomous Astronauts indicates, South London AAA intend to entirely re-invent the concept of what space travel is and can be.

PRESS RELEASE – ISSUED NOVEMBER 1995

The Association of Autonomous Astronauts' independent space-exploration programme, launched on 23 April 1995, includes a 'Five Year Plan' for establishing local, community-based Association of Autonomous Astronauts groups around the world, dedicated to building their own spaceships.

South London Association of Autonomous Astronauts have now announced the dates of their Dreamtime Mission.

After a rigorous training programme, South London AAA

have selected three Autonomous Astronauts who will be in space for a total of 66 hours, from 6 p.m. 21 December 1995 to 12 a.m. 24 December 1995. This mission will therefore coincide with the Winter Solstice.

Due to the secrecy of the mission and the necessity to avoid any interference from the government in this experiment with space travel, specific details of the mission will be kept secret until the press conference is held for the returning Autonomous Astronauts. The location of the conference will be kept a secret until 24 December, but will take place later that day.

South London AAA Dreamtime Mission Statements include these declarations:

- An absolute belief in space as infinite and continuous was conjured up by the inexorable workings of rationality.
- Centuries of psychosocial conditioning maintained by the Hegelian dialectic service a division between inner and outer space.
- Our space travel will destroy the Gnostic concept of an inner space of mind (spirit) that conquers the outer space of the universe (matter).
- Dualism is developed by the military and intelligence agencies as a means of controlling their monopoly on space exploration.
- Knowledge is organised by the state to prevent the working class building their own spaceships.

What we need today is an independent space-exploration programme, one that is not restricted by military, scientific or corporate regulation of the identity of thought and being.

An independent space-exploration programme represents the struggle for emancipatory forms of thinking and being.

The days of this society are numbered.

STATEMENT ISSUED BY THE RETURNING AUTONOMOUS ASTRONAUTS AT A PRESS CONFERENCE IN THE AFTERNOON OF 24 DECEMBER 1995

South London Association of Autonomous Astronauts proclaim the success of their Dreamtime Mission.

At 12 a.m. today, three Autonomous Astronauts from South London AAA returned from space. As part of the Dreamtime Mission we had been in space for a total of 66 hours. The following report attempts to indicate the form that our space travel has taken.

Space-age fictions have enabled us to enter the reality of a new concept of space. This concept formed the working parts for a new form of spacecraft (which we redefined as our concept-craft) which we then constructed using the combined powers of our three minds. Once we had then located the particular orbit our concept-craft was taking around the earth, we simply climbed aboard. We could now move through a new space with the infinite speed of thought. Now we have returned with bloodshot eyes, like revellers after a night of excess, to report our experiences.

For the Dreamtime Mission we had constructed a concept-craft based on a new concept of space. Our new concept of space resists the opinions promoted by government space agencies such as NASA, who want the notion of a divide between inner and outer space. We now have the possibility of creating new concepts of space, concepts that each have their own autonomous existence and philosophical reality, but which still resonate with and connect to other possible concepts.

Like flashes of lightning, our space travel could be defined as a coming and going rather than a tedious advancing from point A to point B and so on. It was certainly more about losing our way than knowing where we were going. And like the lines of flight undertaken by objects floating in zero gravity, the return of one movement of thought would relaunch another, ceaselessly weaving across and throughout this space that we could barely orientate ourselves in. We could see how in this space the most subjective thought is also the most objective.

We inferred that the space we were travelling through was fractal. In addition to this, each movement we made was like the throw of a dice. We were discovering how intuition is important for a space travel that moves by creating connections.

Every movement of thought that passed through the whole of this space did so by immediately turning back on and folding in on itself, like a liquid escaping from gravity. These movements could also fold other movements of thought or allow itself to be folded by them, thereby giving rise to retroactions, connections and proliferations in what we were beginning to discern as an infinitely folded-up infinity that is/was the variably curved space we were travelling in.

To travel through space by means of concepts, at an infinite speed of thought, it is vital to destroy the illusion of a universe that is ours to control. Instead, we move towards the possibilities of connecting with others as we pass from one world to the next. South London AAA are inventors of new immanent modes of space travel and these experimentations of ours are philosophical. The reality of our space travel is not concerned with what we are now but with what we are becoming, which is always different from the present (a present that has already ceased to be).

We have reported our experiences to you and described as best we can something of the form that our space travel takes. More information regarding the specific movements and reactivations of the concept-craft we had constructed for this particular mission must be released at a later date, as we are still compiling the data on this. South London AAA proposes that we construct new concepts of space in order to create emancipatory forms of thinking. The days of this society are numbered.

First published in *Here Comes Everybody! The First Annual Report of the Association of Autonomous Astronauts*, London, April 1996.

ALCHEMICAL INSURRECTION!

Psychedelic Bordigism and the mystical body of
Christ the King

Neoist Alliance

St Paul in his first letter to the Corinthians asserts that men
are endowed by God with a variety of gifts and, using the
metaphor of the human body, remarks how foolish it would
be if one part of the body quarrelled with another part or tried
to opt out of its membership. St Paul insists that this is not
merely an analogy but that human society is actually the body
of Christ. Clearly, this notion is not unrelated to the doctrine of
organic centralism promulgated by the Italian left-communist
Amadeo Bordiga. According to Bordiga, who opposed the
united front tactics of the Communist International, the Party
should consist solely of theoretically coherent militants. After
the accomplished fact of a workers' revolution, the Party was
to become the organ of central administration to human society
– fulfilling a function similar to that of the brain in the human
body.

Rather than being an observation of any merit, the preceding paragraph is merely a parody of the rhetorical technique
employed by Karl Popper in his tedious tirade *The Poverty of
Historicism*. This positivist hack is notorious for his literalism;
he apparently believed that the purpose of historicism was to
predict the future, when anyone who understands Marxist
methodology can see that those propagandists who analysed
cycles of history and then projected these into the future
were attempting to influence the development of the

societies in which they lived through the use of psychological techniques, and suffered very few illusions about the pseudo-scientific status of the discipline they pretended to practise.

While focusing his attacks on similar targets to Popper, in the work *Science, Politics and Gnosticism*, the Christian conservative Erich Voegelin deals at length with what he describes as the 'Gnostic speculation' of Hegel. Through the revival of the immanentism present in Gnostic theology and by identifying divinity entirely with human consciousness, Hegel prepared the way for Marx, Nietzsche and every other modern theorist of merit. The Gnostics replaced a transcendent Deity with the power of illuminated human mind. Hegel, in reanimating this myth under the guise of philosophy, encouraged those who followed in his wake to 'come before Christ and murder love'. While the reactionary Voegelin denounced Hegel's *Phenomenology of Mind* as a sorcerer's handbook, those radicals who have adopted Hegel's method while simultaneously abandoning his system are more than happy to utilise this work as a grimoire.

However, while admiring the restless movement of the Hegelian dialectic, we remain critical of Hegel's conceptual reliance on the *Enneads* of Plotinus and works by Proclus of Athens such as *Institutio Theologica* and *In Platonis Theologiam*. As Voegelin notes, there are parallels between the *Phenomenology* and the movement of the neo-Platonic soul from primordial rest, through alienation and the state of otherness, back through the world towards the soul's alleged source in the so-called unity of the divine being. Rather than seeking a return to unity, a longing that informs the work of every scumbag traditionalist from Papus and Guénon to Julius Evola and Hakim Bey, the Neoist Alliance seeks a higher level of social disintegration. Naturally, this entails the dissolution of those cultural forms that structure this society. Aside from ongoing and unrelenting attacks upon the discourse of philosophy, two of our most immediate targets are those twin phantoms known as the avant-garde and the occult.

While occultists spend a great deal of time faking the antiquity of the activities in which they are engaged, the avant-garde's insistence on the element of innovation within its creations leads to a spurious denial of its historic roots. In this sense, the avant-garde and the occult are two sides of the same coin; they are the positive and negative poles that generate that multifarious enigma known as contemporary society. Since the avant-garde makes itself visible through manifestos, it must be banished. Correspondingly, the occult as a collection of hidden doctrines must be realised (i.e. manifested) if it is to be simultaneously suppressed. The false Hegelianisation of Dada and Surrealism by the Situationist International has long obscured the necessity of this procedure. Since the avant-garde is undesirable, we will vanquish it by uniting it with its polar opposite. By bringing together the avant-garde and the occult (in its Celtic-Druidic form) under the rubric of the avant-bard, the Neoist Alliance is dissolving both these phenomena, and simultaneously destroying the false community engendered by capitalist social relations, a 'social' form predicated on the spectacular opposition of these twin modes of occultural invocation.

Since the Neoist Alliance takes the rhetoric of its opponents and re-orders this verbiage as a means of dissolving ideology, it inevitably follows that certain passive bores believe us to be involved in occult. Nothing could be further from the truth since, as we have already pointed out, to realise the occult is to abolish it. Nevertheless, among those imbeciles who have yet to scale the heights of theoretical incoherence and thereby abandon the illusion of a fixed identity, our activities must remain the night in which all cows are black. Pro-situ hacks and other bourgeois scum are incapable of grasping the passage we are forging between theory and practice. This is not something that can be fixed for ever, but a flow travelling in a very specific direction. Naturally enough, it follows from this that we will not repeat Henry Flynt's error of spending thirty years attempting to frame the 'insight' that 'all beliefs are false' in a manner which is not self-refuting. For us, *belief is the enemy*!

First published in *Re:Action* 3, Winter Solstice 1995.

THE UNACCEPTABLE FACE OF
CONTEMPORARY PSYCHOGEOGRAPHY

London Psychogeographical Association

Whatever doubts we may have about the supersession of art being the 'Northwest Passage' of the geography of real life, we appropriated this image with our Limehouse Rally (22 August, 1993) and revealed how Limehouse served as the location for both Gilbert's original plea to open up the Northwest Passage in 1566, and the IVth Situationist International Conference at the Empire Hostel of the British Sailors Society in September 1960.

The *LPA Newsletter* 3 (Lughnassadh 1993) contained a photo of SI delegates positioned on the Greenwich ley line. In Ralph Rumney's contribution to the Manchester conference – *Some Remarks Concerning the Indigence of Post-Situationists in their Attempts to Recuperate the Past* – he remarks that 'Ley lines went out with Hawksmoor.' We can only take this as a reference to Peter Ackroyd's flawed book which simply bears that architect's name. We would point out to Rumney that Ackroyd's derivative work neither adequately deals with ley lines as theorised by Alfred Watkins in such books as *The Old Straight Track*, nor provides a useful psychogeographical account of Limehouse, particularly in comparison with Iain Sinclair's *Lud Heat*. We would further add that Ackroyd's participation in Gresham College to present a lecture on the former Chosen Chief of the Druids, William Blake, serves to confirm a relationship that we have frequently chronicled in our newsletter. To those who have dismissed our prognostications as the ravings of demented minds, we merely point to the accelerated promotion of former Gresham professor Richard Chartres to the Bishopric of London. To those who simply see the Church of England as an antiquated structure – the Tory party at prayer – we point to a multinational landowner whose operatives, such as Terry Waite and Archbishop Tutu, play key roles in international politics.

The architecture of Canary Wharf illustrates the principles of ley line alignment, which Rumney suggests went out with Hawksmoor three hundred years ago. When an aerial photograph of the principle axis of Canary Wharf is superimposed on an outline of the Mall, the ceremonial approach to Buckingham Palace, the measurements tally precisely. This principle axis is aligned to St Paul's Cathedral, generally recognised as the architectural masterpiece of Sir Christopher Wren. This wretch was the founder of Freemasonry and the Royal Society. The son of the last Register of the Order of the Garter when Charles I was executed, he became a linchpin in the reorganisation of bourgeois society around the restored monarchy of Charles II. Contemporary architecture continues the Masonic patterning of Wren and his acolytes.

We offer no attempt to 'justify' or 'rationalise' the role of magic in the development of our theories; it is sufficient that it renders them completely unacceptable. But the task of reconciling this with the need to offer a fundamental explanation of society has not proved easy. Nevertheless, we have made remarkable progress. For example, the Queen did visit the ley line at Greenwich during an eclipse. We now point to the preparations for the millennium celebrations in Greenwich. Are they preparing a site for ritual king sacrifice where the Canary Wharf Axis crosses the Greenwich peninsular? Will the mythology woven into the landscape allow a re-run of the death of William Rufus? Is Charles being groomed for the role of 'bad king' merely to be executed in a rite that will then strengthen the monarchy?

First published in the leaflet *Sucked: A verification of theses advanced in The Green Apocalypse which demonstrates the sad decomposition of a pro-situ hack*, London, March 1996.

THE JOKER

A Game of Incidental Urban Poker

Workshop for a Non-Linear Architecture

Amongst the various found objects which the *dérive* bestows upon its protagonists, the renegade playing card is a common yet always unexpected gift. The most potent examples usually fall into one of two distinct categories. On the one hand there are those cards whose decayed composition displays a wealth of surface patterning and texture. Such cards, by the nature of their reversion, are frequently so inscribed as to merit inclusion amongst those other found texts or graphic ensembles that illustrate the pages of *The Book of Psychogeography*. Experience has shown that these cards are rare, and to date your author has only come across two such examples during a four-year period of conscious *dérive*.

A much more frequent occurrence however – which both practical experimentation and the laws of probability suggest should account for approximately one half of all cards discovered – is that of the playing card found face down. Such situations are almost always accompanied by an immediate sense of exaggerated anticipation – *which of the fifty-five possibilities have been encountered?* The response can vary, from an immediate desire to turn the card over to a masochistically prolonged pleasure in attempting to envision (in a manner similar to the techniques utilised in co-ordinate visualisation exercises) what might possibly exist on the other side.

In the spring of 1994, during a prolonged series of *dérives* constructed as a consequence of the WNLA instigated *Driftnet* project, a coincidentally large number of such playing cards was discovered. Beginning on a particularly hot and humid April afternoon in the lanes running parallel to the north of the Sauchiehall Street pedestrianised zone (a negative psychogeographic *sink* long since avoided by the navigators of the Glasgow section), a card was discovered lying face down in the dirt beside the stage door of the Theatre Royal. It possessed no particular psychogeographical characteristics at the time of its discovery, primarily because of the exigencies of the constructed *dérive* then being undertaken. The card, a stained and faded three of diamonds, was however incorporated into the documentary findings pertinent to the *dérive*.

The chance encounter of a playing card occurs on average about one in every ten to fifteen *dérives*. (The figure must remain as imprecise as this since no formal statistical analysis has been conducted – the number has been derived purely from anecdotal and remembered experience.) The discovery the next day of another card, again found face down, came therefore as something of a surprise. The card, outside the front door of the Griffinette – the side bar adjacent to the Griffin Pub on King Street – was immediately seized upon and, with a distinct sense of *déjà vu*, cautiously turned over. Its revelation as the four of diamonds immediately shocked the attention of the individual in question, invigorating his imagination with a heightened reverie whose reverberations collided between the nature of such coincidence and the possibilities of discovering a five.

It had long been acknowledged amongst the fluctuating body of WNLA drift participants that encounters with coincidence were one of the more potent, if least understood, reasons for the empowerment of any given *dérive*. An analytical examination of how coincidence operated upon the navigational patterns of the dériving individual had often been suggested, but no one had ever been able to draft even the slightest of coherent texts. The general consensus that finally developed was that those specific coincidences to have played an important role in any given moment or situation of note should be alluded to for the time being only through factual narrative description. The sole exception being the decidedly pataphysical *Third Law of Coincidence*, drafted in the heat of the moment the day before the conclusion of the events now being retold. The Third Law of Coincidence, briefly stated, argues that: 'All coincident moments will be indicative of a notable concurrence of events, suggestive of possessing a resemblant causal interconnection irrespective of whether this is imaginary or actual.'

It should come as no surprise to discover that, following the events of the previous thirty-six hours, our *dérive* protagonist had now all but abandoned the investigations being conducted in response to the *Driftnet* and had set out in search of what to all intents must have appeared the impossible. Upon reflection I suppose the tone of my narrative must have already prepared the reader for the discovery made that evening. The navigator in question was by now using every available technique he possessed in order to locate playing cards, and in such circumstances their discovery must become more likely. It took another full day – the remnants of yesterday being interrupted by persistent reflection – but for the card discovered to be the anxiously sought after five of diamonds is the type of event that the gestating *Third Law of Coincidence* now thrives upon for its verification.

The card was discovered half obscured amongst a collection of left-footed shoes and other discarded items of clothing long since left behind on the traces of St Andrew's labyrinthine lanes. Criss-crossing the floor of the psychogeographical arena beyond the Church's East wall, the tightly interweaving cobbled surfaces were all that remained of one of Glasgow's densest urban quarters. The fact that the card in question was found at twilight, lying face up, should not, I believe, be of any relevance to the intensity of the phenomenon being investigated.

With both the three and the four already tucked away inside his jacket pocket, our incredulous adventurer immediately headed for the Mitre, a small snug of a bar just off Argyll Street and the agreed rendezvous for those intent on our various evening activities. Walking quickly along the darkening backstreets behind the Tron his only goal was to share the marvel of the discovery. The possibilities of finding another playing card, let alone the five of diamonds, had been casually discussed the previous evening, but no one, not even our protagonist, had seriously contemplated its realisation. (It must be remembered here that a *dérive* is never undertaken with the expectation of fulfilling its original premise, but rather of experiencing its natural evolution – of drifting away from the moment of departure in anticipation of the unknown quality of the point of arrival.) Needless to say, following his demonstration of the three cards in the Mitre that evening, the events now being related become almost the only topic of discussion amongst the members of the section, their various associates, friends and collaborators.

The proven integrity of the individual who had made the discoveries fortunately ensured that the debate centred mainly around the nature of coincidence and the consequences of its accidental encounter; the factual content of the discoveries was never brought into question. (The sole exception being that of one canny individual who suggested that half of those present at yesterday evening's session must have spent a good part of the afternoon planting a number of fives of diamonds around the city.) However – although it was the unfolding of the events leading up to the discovery of each card and the role they played in directing or influencing the consequential behaviour of the protagonist that occupied the majority of the discussion – the most potent observation, made quite early on in the evening, was that there lay within this episode the beginnings of a quite remarkable game of Urban Poker.

The hypothesis went as follows:

Two or more drift teams, containing between one and half a dozen navigators, would begin at a given point in time to search for found playing cards. The cards would naturally have to be the genuine 'unsolicited object' (in Breton's sense of the word), although dishonesty in regard of such matters would be left, as is only natural, to the subjective nature of the individual(s) concerned. Initially each team would seek five cards, a number of which (to be decided between the teams in advance) would then be burned, or in other words discarded. Once this agreed number had then been refound, the hand would be brought to a close and publicly declared, e.g. Full House, Pair, Ace High, etc., the winning team being the one with the best hand.

Almost the moment the last words of this explanation had been uttered, the ensemble gathered together erupted in a spontaneous chorus of approval, suggestion, variation and counterproposal. The idea had definitely taken hold, but then again once the mind had begun to explore the possible consequences then so it should have. And this was precisely what our navigator had begun to do. His inquisitive nature had already started speculating as to how to encourage the evolution of this newly emergent *dérive* ever since the jubilation of picking up the five had begun to fade away. Even while returning from St Andrew's, cards in hand, our navigator had entertained the notion that an alternative set of moves would now be required.

Lets face it, the actual discovery of a six had never stood a chance and any attempt even to begin searching for it had been discarded from the outset. Even the most cursory of calculations posited the chances of success at $1/(55)^4$ – or roughly one in about 9 million – and even that calculation clearly ignored a whole host of other variables. Somehow, the impossibility of discovering the five had contained within it the consciously understood knowledge of the chance of success, and it was that glimpse of the possible that had enabled the card to be sought – not necessarily found, but definitely looked for. With the introduction of the idea of a game of Urban Poker it appeared that this necessary redirecting of the *dérive* had begun.

So as the commotion in the bar subsided, it was our navigator, closely followed by the originator of the idea, who were seen to move away towards the back of the room. Their intention was to transcribe the contents of the conversation, to put everything down on paper before it was passed over and eventually forgotten. (Sadly enough it would not have been the first time that such a brainwave had been allowed to slip away into the mists of an ever-fading memory.) Between the two of them each proposal was considered, analysed and either rejected or co-opted into what was rapidly becoming a coherent ludic structure. Time passed by and the evening seemed to slip away quickly. The conversation ebbed with the pennies that had fuelled it until finally the last half heavy brought our two conspirators back to the agenda at hand: the midnight excursion into Bremner's basement and the first group penetration of the *Inside Outside*. The *Inside Outside* was a Victorian backstreet 'time warp', a spatial ambience that had been completely entombed for well over a century. It had recently been exposed by a local surveying company who, after months of trying to understand the building's complex maze of walls, floors, tunnels and basements, had finally got around to prizing open the various light wells and air shafts concealed inside.

As the dawn light welcomed the following morning, a host of entirely external circumstances now prevented our navigator from pursuing any further *dérive* activity – a state of affairs that would last well into Thursday afternoon. The chain of events immediately surrounding the discovery of the cards appeared to have been broken. In fact it wasn't until the following Wednesday, after a chance encounter the previous evening between the protagonist and the originator, that further progress was to be made. The two of them had agreed to meet up, appropriately enough considering the nature of the subject matter in hand, on the desolate, overgrown island in the middle of the Port Dundas canal loop. This now partially forested waste ground, previously one of Glasgow's busiest ports, was only accessible by climbing precariously along the undercarriage of the single bridge that connected the island with the surrounding area. The gates, side fence and various security bars were not only physically inaccessible, but liberally covered with a malevolent anti-climb paint. No one, however, had the foresight to imagine that an attempt to gain access to the island would be made via the underside of the bridge!

The crossing took about twenty minutes, but once ashore both of them headed immediately for the south side of the island, to a concrete jetty immediately beyond which, just below the surface of the water, lay a rusted wreck of a car with the word 'joker' sprayed across the roof. It was in this setting that the two of them had decided to draft – not conclusively, but sufficient enough for the inaugural game to commence – *The Rules of Urban Poker*.

Despite remaining as close as possible to the original hypothesis, a number of variations upon the initial theme were agreed. The first, and definitely the most interesting, was that the game should be undertaken between different cities. The playing off of one urban entity against another, and the possible transprogrammatic consequences offered by the circumstantial spatial juxtapositioning involved, had evoked considerable enthusiasm. Without concretely appreciating what this might eventually entail, both of them were convinced of its future potential. A game of five-card stud was started on 7 June 1996 between WNLA London, 391 Paris, FluxAlba and Beirut F-ART, with the specific aim of developing these possibilities.

A decision was also made to underline firmly the fact that the cards were not to be deliberately sought. If Breton's criteria for the *objet insolite* were to be held to then the cards would have to give themselves both willingly and unexpectedly to the players of the game. Our navigator had already expressed the opinion that the actual search for the five, as opposed to its discovery, had not been entirely satisfactory and that had he not found anything that day it would have been an extremely frustrating experience. It was his view that an unexpected chance encounter and the sudden reaquaintance of the participant with the ongoing game – despite the obvious increase in game duration – would prove far more satisfying.

Thirdly, it was agreed that rather than various drift teams, a single individual, operating in each city, would lend the game a more distinctly interpersonal character. It's not that teams of individuals in each city were considered erroneous, rather it was more a case of the Glasgow section's relations with other cities at that time involving only individuals, as opposed to groupings, who would be likely to play the game. More pertinent, however, was that our navigating protagonist, after finding three cards of such quality in so short a space of time, was determined to complete the task of locating his hand alone, and that in such circumstances it would be appropriate to pit his discoveries against those made by other like-minded individuals. Team attempts were perfectly plausible for future games, but with this one already half-completed by a single individual, its essence should be maintained.

The only other real change to the original theme was that, rather than waiting until the first five cards had been located, each find should be communicated directly to the opponent(s) involved; the reason being that this would intensify the sense of ongoing participation with the overall unfolding of the game. It was suggested that such a move might encourage dishonesty, but with this question having already been resolved by the decision to accept the word of all participating navigators right from the outset, the suggestion was held to be irrelevant. And so, with continuity of participation being held to be far more important than the irritable subjectivity of apparent truth, the only course of action was to let the game commence.

Previously issued as a privately circulated pamphlet.

ORDERS OF DEATH

The Western intelligence services viewed as an occult conspiracy

Neoist Alliance

When one asks the average tabloid reader to name the largest and most powerful occult group active in the world today, the answer might be anything from the OTO (Ordo Templi Orientis) to the Pagan Federation. In reality, despite the boost such operations are frequently given by media exaggerations of their influence, these groups are pitifully small. Likewise, many right-wing conspiracy theorists see the Illuminati as the most powerful mystical movement at work within the contemporary world, despite the fact that this particular order was effectively suppressed in the eighteenth century!

More sophisticated veterans of the occult and conspiracy scenes might come closer to the truth by suggesting the Masons or the Papacy as bodies of occult significance. Surprisingly few people seem to share our view that the largest and most powerful occult organisation currently orchestrating events on the world stage is the Anglo-American intelligence octopus, which cannot be reduced to simply being the CIA or MI6. Of course, there is internal rivalry between the British and American security services, just as on this side of the pond much jostling for position goes on between MI5 and MI6. Nevertheless, the important fact is that these are internal family arguments, and this institutionalised rivalry is a means of solving the problems associated with transmitting directives from the hierarchy to field operatives, in what would otherwise be a huge organisation utterly crippled by bureaucracy.

Millions of people are familiar with books such as *Satan and Swastika*, *Occult Reich*, *The Nazis and the Occult*, *Hitler and the Age of Horus* and *The Occult Roots of Nazism*. The idea that Himmler's SS was an occult order is popular among fringe historians, although most academics try to steer clear of such notions. Obviously, university-based researchers would incur the wrath of their paymasters if they immersed themselves too deeply in the wide range of technical problems associated with ruling the world.

The Neoist Alliance does not, of course, wish to suggest that the majority of college professors consciously participate in a conspiracy orchestrated by the power elite. It should go without saying that, for a conspiracy to function effectively, the number of those consciously operating on its behalf ought to be kept to a bare minimum. The rules that govern what is academically acceptable, and in particular methodological compartmentalisation, result in the majority of successful academics being completely unaware of whose interests they really serve.

Given the influx of Nazi personnel into Anglo-American military and scientific circles after the Allied victory, it's surprising how little has been written by occult and conspiracy researchers about the possible effects this had on the more esoteric aspects of the CIA's modus operandi. Neoist Alliance activists could easily churn out paperbacks with titles such as *Satan and the CIA* or *Lucifer and Lenin*, if they were at all interested in carving out careers for themselves as the authors of mass-market books. Turning to British intelligence, we find in John Dee a key figure in the founding of both the modern espionage system and contemporary occultism. Like Aleister Crowley, Dee used occultism as a cover for his intelligence activities.

Moving forward several centuries, we have just been confronted with a key episode in the ongoing organisation of appearances, that is to say the ruling elite's preferred method of mind control, the spectacle. The occult has always operated as a rhetorical system, or, put another way, as a system of symbol manipulation, and the media had a field day with the spectacle presented by the mass death of members of the Luc Jouret cult. Beneath a welter of irrelevant and contradictory facts, the masses were enticed to imbibe yet again the moral fable that both personal happiness and collective safety lie solely in strict conformity to the velvet diktats of the power elite.

It comes as no surprise that on the same day the press broke the story of the 'Alpine Armageddon', we were also treated to headlines such as *College Hypnotist Created Zombies* (this particular formulation is from *The Times* of 6 October 1994). The news that two seventeen-year-olds from York College were taken to hospital when staff found they couldn't wake them from a trance induced by a fellow student, served to reinforce the fact that we are all victims of media mind control. It should not need stating that the media is simply the mass outreach department of the security services.

Journalism has been persistently exposed as one of the main covers for spooks gathering data in the field, and also as a highly effective conduit for propaganda and disinformation. The Neoist Alliance is not suggesting that everyone who works in the media is a spook; that would be both counterproductive and inefficient. The intelligence services simply place their operatives in key posts so that they can create standards of 'professionalism' that result in the vast majority of journalists promoting the interests of the secret state while barely being conscious of its existence.

Returning briefly to Jouret, every newspaper story gave a different interpretation of the symbolism associated with the various coloured robes his dead followers were wearing. This was, of course, an irrelevance, since the symbolic significance of clothing is of little interest to those outside the cult. More interestingly, the press appeared incapable of correctly naming the organisation that Jouret led, eventually settling on the title Order of the Solar Temple. The correct English translation, at least according to Gaetan Delaforge in his book *The Templar Tradition in the Age of Aquarius* (Putney, Vermont, 1987), is International Order of Chivalry, Solar Tradition.

However, getting hung up on Jouret, and whether or not he is really dead, is to step into the trap sprung by the intelligence bureaucracy. The names and biographical details of the individuals who actually assassinated the likes of JFK and MLK are irrelevant; what is important is the overall movement of the interlinked conspiracies fighting for control of the world. By stepping outside the immediate field of play, it becomes possible to grasp the unfolding of the power elite's geopolitical machinations. Those who have done so long ago realised that, like Lee Harvey Oswald, both the tramps and Clay Shaw were also decoys.

The Neoist Alliance is bored in the city; there is no longer any Temple of the Sun. Real life lies elsewhere, in the simultaneous realisation and suppression of the Masonic system adhered to by the ruling elites of a world we will shortly leave behind as we ascend to the Sun.

First published in *Re:Action* 1 Winter Solstice 1994.

THE TRUTH ABOUT THE BATAVIAN REVOLUTION

Anti-Euclidean Action

Batavia was founded in 1619 as the privileged spot of the Dutch trade in the East Indies. It provided one omphalos of an elliptical world-wide web of trade and exchange that constituted the Dutch empire. The other was Amsterdam. This empire had been built on the Phoenician model, and Bonrepaus accused the Dutch of having built their fortune 'upon the ruins of the Europeans who had proceeded them, taking advantage of the trouble others had taken to civilise the Indians, to domesticate them and give them the taste for commerce'. This was not the site of the Batavian Revolution.

Batavia was founded in 1802 in Genese County, New York, on the Tonawanda Creek. It is eleven miles from Attica. It gained world-wide prominence as the home of William Morgan when he threatened to reveal Masonic Secrets in the Batavian Republican Advocate, 1826. His subsequent disappearance led to the formation of the Anti-Masonic Party. This party was the focus of anti-Masonic propaganda that led to the reduction of the number of Masons in New York state from 20,000 to 3,000 by the early 1830s. This was not the site of the Batavian Revolution.

Batavia is a poetic name for the Netherlands derived from the ancient Germanic tribe called the Batavi, whose district was centred around Lugdunum, now known as Leiden. It was here that John Toland came to study in the late seventeenth century. However it was in the 1780s that the Batavian Revolution took place. Following a Prussian invasion Leiden eventually capitulated to the Prussian troops on 10 October 1787. This precipitated a violent and systematic reaction as Orange mobs loyal to the Stadtholder, William V, systematically murdered their opponents. Thousands of revolutionaries fled, including the twin brothers Florian and Florithe Cramer.

The Cramer twins had been leading figures during intense discussions that took place in the lead up to the Batavian Revolution. Central to these discussions was the role of the word 'the'. This word is defined as definition defining itself. Hence it is called the definite article. It only exists in the present tense as the and the gerund, thing. The is usually regarded as the fourth word in the English lexicon after a, be and see. This has, however, been attributed to a confusion between its original spelling with a 'thorn', a disused letter unavailable in this font, but which looked like a 'd' with a cross on the high stroke. This letter was pronounced 'th' and was later debased to 'y', as in 'ye olde tea shop'. Here the 'y' was always pronounced 'th' until it dropped from use. It only attained a 'y' pronunciation when the spelling was revived as an anachronism.

Of course, during the seventeenth century there was a party who maintained that the was the first word in the English lexicon, quoting the testament of St John: 'In the beginning was the'. These people, called Theists, held that the universe began with definition defining itself, and that definition existed outside time but without definition. This was contested by the Anists who in their 'Several Indefinite Articles of Faith' promulgated a more intuitive approach. The Anists suggested that definition must have been not only without definition but also, in fact, indefinite. This current quickly fragmented into a variety of sects who all maintained some, but not all, of the 'Several Indefinite Articles of Faith' of the founding Synod. One faction, the Atheists tried to develop a compromise, arguing that it was impossible to have definition without indefinition, and that the two were yoked together. They reasserted all the 'Several Indefinite Articles of Faith' but declared these to be 'The Indefinite Articles of Faith' to which they added 'Several Definite Articles of Faith' which embodied many of the 'Theses of the Theists'.

Unfortunately, this stimulating debate was brought to a halt with the suppression of the Batavian Revolution and the execution of nearly all of the participants. The only survivor was a certain Florian Cramer, who established a dynasty that has continued this debate amongst all his descendants. As Cramer established a tradition of calling all his children Florian Cramer, a habit that they have maintained to this day, much of this modern debate between the several hundred Florian Cramers now living is almost impossible for an outsider to unravel. Should an investigator enquire whether a particular Florian Cramer is the Florian Cramer responsible for a particular tract, the response will not so much depend on a correct or incorrect identity, but rather on the position of the particular individual in the debate.

There has been an ongoing debate as to whether Florian Cramer is a theist or the theist. What is certain is that they do not wear Orange under any circumstances. This dates from the time when either the original Florian Cramer or simply a Florian Cramer fled from the Orange reaction following the Batavian Revolution, when everyone was forced to wear the Orange colours. The opposition put up some resistance, arranging their cockades into a 'V' for *vrijheid*, Dutch for Freedom. This V sign was subsequently used by the British as V for victory during the Second World War.

Strictly speaking, Florithe Cramer did not take part in the the debates, of which he is not a chronicler (or the chronicler, depending on which school you follow). Like his twin brother, he escaped the suppression of the Batavian Revolution and went to live in Antrim, where he subsequently participated in the Battle of Antrim. He did so by gathering the Dulse of Folly. Dulse is a local variety of edible seaweed which is gathered in summer to be consumed in great quantities at the Lammas fair in Bally castle. The Dulse of Folly was seaweed gathered on the shores of Rathlin Island. According to ancient Irish legend, those who consume this dulse are liberated from weighty ideas and are able to enjoy life to the full, untroubled by pointless disputes.

Just before the Turnout, Florithe Cramer visited Rathlin Island and harvested the crop of the Dulse of Folly, even though the season had not reached full term. His plan was to distribute the dulse to insurgents and militiamen alike, as he favoured neither faction, and saw their conflict simply as a source of bloodshed. He conveyed the material by blockwheel cart along the Moyle Way to Carnlough, where he took the road to Ballymena. Along this road he fell in with a group of United Irishmen. Whereas he could not induce them to partake of any dulse, they, however, bearing the advantage of being armed, induced him to secrete various pikes in and amongst the seaweed, and sent him out before them. Although he turned off the high road, in the village of Buckna he was accosted by some yeomen, who were filled with a desire to search his car, fearing precisely the deception that the United Irishman had carried out. However, their commander was a Ballycastle man with a particular fondness for dulse, and before the pikes were found had already arranged for some to be prepared for him. He was sitting at the kitchen table of a local farm with the plate of dulse before him when Cramer was dragged in and nine pike heads thrown down on the ground as evidence of Cramer's subversive activity. The commander, deeming that Cramer could wait a few moments while he devoured the dulse, kept our poor hero waiting. This was to save Cramer's life. Having consumed the dulse, Cramer's profuse if vague explanation that he was a Quaker, and had no inkling as to how the pike heads secreted themselves amongst the dulse, was readily accepted.

Cramer then fled up Slemish mountain, a local peak, to seek refuge. Some yeomen, despairing of their commander's softened attitude, still held out hope for the fifteen-shilling bounty offered for each corpse of a dead insurgent. They pursued Cramer up the mountain, until they happened on a group of Jack Fullarton's men who had also sought refuge there. Having been inspired by greed rather than bravery, the yeomen fled when it became apparent that they would be resisted. However, the insurgents were most put out that Cramer had neglected to scoop up the pike-heads when he had fled from Buckna, and were on the point of doing him some serious injury when Captain Fullarton returned from Ballymena. Fullarton had the foresight to gain the rank of captain amongst both the United Irishmen and the Volunteers. After he had been betrayed by Andrew Swann (who was subsequently hanged by his neighbours upon a sallagh tree), Fullarton had ridden to the headquarters of the militia to negotiate a pass for himself and his followers so that they could proceed unmolested to Derry and thence to the United States of America.

Florithe Cramer was thus passing through the village of Clogh on his way to Derry, when he saw the military subjecting an old man by the name of Esler to fifty lashes for some unspecified misdemeanour. After thirty lashes had been administered, Esler fainted. This incident touched Cramer, who, carried away by an altruistic impulse, at once threw off his coat and begged to be allowed to receive the remaining twenty lashes, instead of the old man. His selfless behaviour was taken as evidence of his leadership among the Insurrectionists and it was therefore deemed necessary to make an example of him. Notwithstanding his pass, he was arrested, conveyed to Ballymena, tried by court martial and sentenced to be hanged.

The death of Florithe Cramer was dramatic. It was at first decided that he should suffer on the Moat, but in deference to Cramer's own wishes, a nearby hazel tree was decided upon, and he was conveyed there by cart. When all the arrangements for the final scene were completed, he attempted to address the multitude who had gathered to witness his last moments. He said 'If all had tried some of the Dulse of Folly which I had brought from Raithlin Island,' when a dozen muskets were levelled at him, and cries of 'silence,' and 'drive on the cart' arose from those assembled to see the dread sentence fulfilled. He met his fate with an unsubdued spirit. His body, after hanging a sufficient length of time, was taken to a wall alongside the Castle, and then hung in chains over the moat. However, the weight of the corpse was too great for the pins by which the chains were fastened to the wall. They broke away from the wall and the body slid down into the river where a giant salmon swam up and devoured Florithe Cramer's body in one gulp.

Some dispute Florithe Cramer's existence, claiming that there is no record of Florian Cramer having a twin brother before the suppression of the Batavian Revolution. They have even suggested that Florithe was a name simply adopted by Florian when he went to Antrim. Here different schools of thought offer different explanations, some maintaining that it was the Florian Cramer, of whom Florithe is supposedly the twin brother; others that it was simply another Florian Cramer, a son of the Florian Cramer, whose contribution to the Battle of Antrim led to such a grisly end at Ballymena Castle.

John Toland's sojourn in Leiden in the early eighteenth century provided a link with both the Presbyterian currents of Northern Ireland and Harringtonian Republicanism, which arose in the English Revolution. At one and the same time, he conveyed the central tenets of Newtonian mechanics and materialist thought to French émigré circles there, and, through such secret societies as the Knights of Jubilation, texts were smuggled into France. The Batavian Revolution saw these seeds, planted some seventy years earlier, reach fruition. Although the revolution was viciously stamped out by the Prussian army, it nevertheless did as much to lay the groundwork for the French Revolution as events in America.

Orange reaction has its fountainhead in the Roman Theatre to be found in Orange, a small town in France. This theatre, as the best preserved surviving Roman theatre, embodies all the occult features that Palladio tried to revive in his four books on architecture. The founder of Freemasonry, Sir Christopher Wren, used these principles in the construction of the Sheldonian Theatre, Oxford, which is still used for the rituals surrounding the awarding of degrees and other qualifications. William V of Orange was the Stadtholder, when the Orange mobs ran amok following the demise of the Batavian Revolution. Since then, the current of orange reaction has spread across Northern Ireland and penetrated southern Africa where an 'Orange Free State' was founded.

Those who don't learn from history are condemned to repeat it. Thus it is of the essence that the lessons of the Batavian Revolution are assimilated immediately to ensure that we do not drown in a sea of orange reaction.

Previously unpublished.

FOR A WORLD WITHOUT PRICKS

Gruppe M

While they have extensively researched their own area of interest, most conspiracy theorists are unfamiliar with scientific methodology. Nevertheless, the rhetoric of conspiracy 'researchers' is quasi-scientific. Their conjectures are supported with apparently 'logical' links that are forged between divergent 'occult' forces. Conspiracy theory is essentially masculine. The male only feels fulfilled under the bright light of day, where he is duly protected thanks to his acceptance of government and power. Here, the intuitive knowledge of the moon goddess, fundamental to all ancient religions, is viewed as castration. Christian sects transformed the gods of rival religions into devils who threatened patriarchal order with feminine irrationality. The dark powers exposed by the conspiracy 'researcher' include witches, alchemists, Gnostics, Templars, Illuminoids, Jacobites, Freemasons, rootless cosmopolitan elements, state assets, neo-Nazis, communists and Satanists.

The conspiracy theorist has been infantalised. He comes across as having spent his entire life devouring novels by the likes of Alexander Dumas, Arthur Conan Doyle and Robert Louis Stevenson. Conspiracy theorists fabricate adventure stories about hidden powers manipulating events played out on the theatre of the world. It should go without saying that the claims of conspiracy 'researchers' can never be verified. The conspiracy theorist plays at being a detective. He acts like a paranoid child who does not understand that there is no simple explanation for complex social phenomena. According to Freud, the male infant discovers he can live without the penis. The paranoid petit-bourgeois longs for completed castration. The fulfilment of his theories, if this were possible, would result in the death of the conspiracy 'researcher'. Fear of castration produces a desire for oppression, a deep longing for impotence and passivity in the masses. The neurotic suffers from self-inflicted denial; in other words, he is a masochist. Conspiracy theory offers the neurotic the possibility of escape from the mundane world of things as they are.

Valerie Solanas stood Freud on his head. She claimed that men are incomplete women. Men want to be active, but they are passive and long to be female. Conspiracy 'researchers' desire castration but are unable to realise this longing. Conspiracy theorists see the prick as a synonym of power. Ironically, those who think in this manner are already dickless. In the *economy of desire* where everything is centred on the individual, the repressively driven conspiracy 'researcher' celebrates in *angst* the loss of an object he has never possessed. The phallus is a possession of the sun god and the state. Everything else is merely religious revolt on the part of romantics hallucinating pain in a phantom limb. Fear of castration is actually a longing for castration. The paranoid male transforms real desire into a symbolic representation; he creates a conspiracy theory. The greatest desire of the impotent male is to unmask others. It gives him a false sense of power.

Loosely translated and ruthlessly abridged from the German. The full German text appeared in *Sklvaen* 30, Berlin, 1997.

METASTASIS

Genetics and Ideology

Matthew Fuller

Cancer is the runaway growth of cells and as such is the most truly spontaneous upsurge of creativity that a human being is capable of. Cancer is *the* threat to post-industrial Western society and comes from a completely unexpected quarter: the body, the terrain most ensnared by the authoritarian net.

Nature has taken it upon itself to supersede the present order. Revolutionary proletarians should therefore encourage the growth of cancer in their bodies. We must fight against the capitalist recuperation of the creative cell. Don't let the rich get it all.

Cancer is a betrayal from within. Cells that were hitherto 'law-abiding citizens' change their properties, begin to divide and grow without reference to the needs of the organism, invade adjacent normal tissues, and may even spread to other parts of the body and form equally lawless secondary deposits (metastases). These anarchic centres may be set up in almost any organ. (They provide the exception to the generalisation about the inverse relationship between differentiation and the power to divide.) It is one of the characteristics of the growth of cancer cells that the normal cells that turn to malignancy tend to lose their differentiation. The faster they grow and divide, the more primitive they become.

THE SYSTEM GIVES WITH ONE HAND AND SNATCHES BACK WITH THE OTHER

Of course in this world, the best of all possible worlds, we are offered the chance to induce cancer, if we buy the correct products: cigarettes, cars, nuclear power systems. The measurement of creative possibility in terms of the power to purchase results in a fetishisation, not of the unconsciously desired state of encanceration but of its symbolic replacement.

However, not only does the system provide, it also takes away – in amazing feats of raw blackmail, with billboards, magazine articles, and advertisements placed by organisations with such overly colonising names as the Imperial Cancer Research Fund. The ruling hegemony produces in workers the fear that if they do not part with enough money (collectively with millions) to keep thousands of highly paid specialists in their accustomed luxury laboratories then one in ten to one in three (figures vary) of them will experience not the truly joyful biochemical liberation inherent in us all, but being smitten down with a mythic evil, second not even to demons of their more ancient mystifications. In such a way has the proletariat been seduced by its own sterilisation.

HEALTH: THE BODY FRAGMENTED

By turning Law into a permanent Fun Run, capital pushes every proletarian into the front line of their own repression. The capitalist propagation of 'health' can be understood in its undistorted essence when it becomes the universal category of society as a whole. Proletarians with the merest amount of revolutionary consciousness will realise that, in a world that really is topsy-turvy, the moment of purest health is the moment of death. Only in this context does the alienation produced by health assume decisive importance for the objective evolution of society and for the stance adopted by the people towards it. Health is the technical realisation of cellular creativity exiled into a beyond; it is separation perfected within the interior of person. The proletarian is displaced from her own body, inhabiting instead a model that functions with perfect replication but not with process. Health is the reactionary conditioning that has its ancestry in the total programmed repetition of Pavlov. This most surely marks the departure from capitalism as something outside of the body, a structural relationship between separate cell masses, into that of a field which, slipped in between pores, insinuates a new terrain, the body politic materialised. However refracted, reflected and segmented the body may be within the prevailing conditions of production and consumption's hall of mirrors, these relations are now trapped within something that escapes their logic. The projected unification of society in the amniotic fluid of separation serves only to increase the atomisation of its vital cellular fabric.

THE RESPONSE OF THE LEFT

Even when such establishment figures as John Wayne manage to overcome the generations of conditioning mangling their bodies, by a suitable exposure to radioactivity in a nuclear testing site, the laughing hyenas of the traditional left hoot with derision. That the Duke himself was able to achieve this ultimate of revolutionary praxis, without any significant ideological shift, points to this as being the most potent, and in the long term only viable, agent of change. Unable through rigid orthodoxy to accept the genetic directives for even their own internal liberation, they seek instead to strangle this rupturing feast with a bureaucracy that unless entirely mechanised contains the hidden flower of freedom. The health policies of all the present and would-be cellular Gestapo reveal only different straps of the same straining truss.

The primary event in the encanceration of a cell is a mutation within a normal somatic cell, the gene or genes affected are those that directly or indirectly are responsible for cell division. Cancer has to be the result of such a mutation. The transmission of the cell to the ecstasy of revolutionary transfiguration is therefore only possible in the most normal of conditions. The reactionary nature of those who attempt to build a revolution is in direct proportion to the extent of their abnormal fervour.

WHAT IS TO BE DONE?

As a first step towards freedom, the proletariat should seize the means of cancer production. A nuclear power station under the control of the international working class would be able to provide a fair share of radioactive isotopes for all. That the spirit of 1917 still lives on in Russia should be clear to all after the historic liberation of thousands of revolutionary isotopes by the workers of Chernobyl. Critical theory must *contaminate* with its own language. The tongues of theoreticians must realise their inherent carcinogeneity. A hermeneutics of revolutionary genetics must be formed in order to formulate the immediate and spontaneous encanceration of the proletarian body.

THE FUTURE

This text, and its inevitable victorious climaxing of the class struggle, undoubtedly marks a crucial breakthrough in human understanding. However, this co-carcinogenesis is only a preliminary stage. The creation of cancer must eventually be released from any form of mediation whatsoever. Cancer is the purest form of maverick creativity present on this planet. Speculation has been made as to whether the brains of all animal life are not merely the degenerated remains of once glorious tumours, atrophied into cruel parodies after thousands of years of the historical descent into capitalism. The eventual forms of our liberation will only become apparent as genetic imperatives combine with the practical possibilities we create for them. Released from bondage, who knows the extent of the full beauty of the blossom. Forward the independent creative cell.

First published in *Leisure* 3, Cardiff 1989.

CHRONICLE OF THE NEOAST OBSERVER AT THE SO-CALLED MILLIONTH APARTMENT FESTIVAL

John Fare

My arrival in NYC was dissatisfying. I had intended to leave Baltimore blindfolded but was unable to find a travelling companion and so made the journey sighted and alone. When I arrived in the city I took the subway to the Lower East Side, where I waited on the street for several hours, trying to make contact with members of the Neoast Cultural Conspiracy and other friends by telephone; trying to find a place to piss or drop off my bags (including my 'Mental Case' – a bag formed from a convoluted straitjacket). On the street I was repeatedly offered crack and a piece of ass and directions. I gave up trying to find shelter and went to the Rivington Sculpture Garden at 6 p.m., where the first public event of the festival was scheduled to take place: a Neoast bonfire. The Garden is a lot taken over by metal constructions, salvage and debris assembled by members of the Rivington School. The Rivington School is a 'street-nationalist' group (from Rivington Street), peripherally in league with a Karen Eliot.

When I arrived, the Garden was dark and a few people were shooting drugs inside – with what appeared to be a cursory attempt at secrecy. I didn't recognise them and decided to circle round the block, past another small party where some people were laughing and shoving each other around. A few false recognitions on the street later I found Neoasts had arrived in the Sculpture Garden. They were lighting the camp-fire under some crates. Present were Theresa Rodrigues and her boyfriend Allen, Torontonians Ottelie and her boyfriend Gordon W. Zealot, a Karen Eliot, Cowboy Ray Kelley of the Rivington School, Matty Jankowski, a person called Jeffrey and a few whose names I didn't hear. Introductions were made in a festive atmosphere with various people standing on a crate placed on top of the fire. Ottelie was the longest lasting fire walker, perched a few feet in the air with the flames licking around her feet. Gordon W. played an Indian Kohl Drum with considerable volume as a Karen Eliot sang what were presumably Hungarian folk songs, and I beat on the metal sculptures around a nonplussed audience. A Karen Eliot pro-claimed that 'at Rivington, it is always six o'clock', which was repeatedly expressed throughout the festival.

The German anti-Neoast Stiletto arrived shortly after, carrying an intervolometer. Other projections of the Baltimore Neoast Contingency – Peter Zahorecz, Debbie Montgomery-Glen, tENTATIVELY a cONVENIENCE and the formidable Jamaica – arrived and discussed with those present the impounding of Debbie's car, which had been relocated by the police to an area of the city where they were more certain of their sovereignty. This event left them with no certain way of returning to Baltimore. Conversations then ensued, during which Peter presented me with a French 'verb-finding wheel' from his special Berlitz Case, and I broke out a body-piercing magazine for general viewing. Photographs of the distended labia of 'Mistress Noni' generated some comment among the assembled hangers-on. Theresa seemed inflamed by the idea of being a participant in such marginal somatic alterations. Gordon W. then promised to introduce me to the logician and former associate of Fluxus, Henry Flynt, sometime during the festival.

Peter Zahorecz cut the sterile bandages that I had brought from Baltimore and taped them to my eyes with medical tape, over which he fastened a tight blindfold. I am indebted to him for his help. The result of his labour was blindness that endured for the rest of the festival, though the blindfold was restored and the bandages replaced daily to avoid eye infection. I could barely perceive changes in illumination from daylight to darkness. From then on, I gave each person I met a numbered ticket imprinted with the legend 'active participant and impartial observer' and a different number, in order to clarify the roles involved in my meeting them. I agreed with Stiletto to serve as blind cameraman for sections of his autobiographical film *The Prodigal Son*. I was then led through a tunnel of fires in the garden. The flames were immense in 'my' mind. Theresa expressed some anxiety about my safety during the festival, but a Karen Eliot assured her that I made 'this kind of *violent* performance all the time'. On the street, sections of Stiletto's film were shot whenever I 'saw' anything that interested me.

The next event of the festival consisted of dinner in a Polish restaurant with Peter and Stiletto – a loose conference to adjust the present personalities. Instinctively I realised that perogies were – at least temporarily – to displace chapatis as a primary Neoast foodstuff, and so I ordered and ate them. The best technique turned out to be putting each one into my mouth whole and trying to salvage the grease and sour cream with my tongue. Throughout the festival I relied on the falsely evoked sympathy of waiters, who assumed my eyes had been damaged in an accident and were extremely polite.

That night a vaudeo-evening styled as *Catholic Convulsion* took place in the Chameleon Club, where participants of the festival assembled to drink and stand or sit in proximity to a large vaudeo-projection. After some whoopala, tENTATIVELY presented vaudeo, with the eleven-month old Jamaica giving a live commentary, which was amplified via contact mike. tENTATIVELY encouraged hecklers to get on stage and participate via microphones, and then scolded them for being cowards when they didn't do so. Some members of the 'audience' responded angrily to the combination of a 'baby' and tENT's *sex and vomit-drenched* public service message vaudeo. Others responded by directly stimulating my body with their hands, clothing, mouths, tongues, asses, backs, legs, beards, breath and breasts. At the time, this sexual stimulation was so prolonged, intense and omnidirectional that I couldn't tell how many people of which genders were engaging me, although I enjoyed this increase in my disorientation.

At least one time people were standing on a table. Various other vaudeos, including a presentation from Richard Martel, ensued in a general atmosphere of anarchy that bordered on normalcy. I assumed I was in the midst of the 'fundamental vulgarity of the Rivington School'. We were invited by a Karen Eliot to spend at least a night of the festival sleeping in the window of her apartment. Peter, tENT and I readily accepted this idea, but never carried it through.

I slept that night in the apartment of the Unknown Neoast, who was appropriately unaware of our presence in her domicile as she was away. The accommodation had been arranged by another Neoast and we were advised to take full precautions to conceal ourselves. Elaborate traps were set by the door and in the halls to kill or detain the apartment's owner should she arrive prematurely to find all nine of us in occupation like Bedouins. The next day a complex command-centre was set up to co-ordinate the activities of the festival, with additional telephones and continuous mail-delivery.

Debbie spoke (in a disembodied voice) of her ability to pick up radio transmissions with her metal fillings. I began to feel major psychical changes as a result of my visual depravation – depression, introversion, a lost sense of the lapsing of time. We were on the street and met with Gordon W., Theresa and others. Somehow we had left the apartment and ended up at the Stockwell Gallery, a structure like a firehouse on the outside, and with an interior resembling a Byzantine chapel hung with cloth partitions. I began to hallucinate steadily. I distributed texts which were added to a wall of Neoast *paraganda*. tENTATIVELY crouched next to me on the floor and asked me to sign a contract (which I couldn't see) with my blood. I agreed and he cut my finger with a Swiss-Army knife. Then I was told that the contract legally ensured that I would loan him twenty dollars every day for the remainder of the festival.

Further Neoast spectacles were being enacted and vaudeos shown, while Gordon W. prepared an Indian meal for all present. The majority of the previous night's belligerents and more were apparently circulating in the room, where I socialised with vigour, feeling ecstatic and surrounded in invisible and pulsing space. A 'collective' Neoast book was in progress, with pages strewn across the floor and on the walls. Stiletto filmed me commenting on the works hung in the gallery, which I could not see. Many introductions were made and more benign sexuality was felt. Theresa Rodrigues and I planned to pierce each other's spinal columns as a mutual introduction to surgical body-play, and she agreed to search for suitable rings before the next night's events. We rallied to sleep at the apartment of the Unknown Neoast. Flaming skulls, tentacles, worms, ice, metal, night-sticks, windows, sheets, numbers, distilleries, teeth and other objects were locked in orbit around my head, which was like smoke.

I remember almost nothing clearly from the next day except trying to navigate in the apartment. My psychological state had deteriorated and I found it difficult to pull myself out of my disorientation enough to do anything. In the apartment, plans were being made to retrieve the impounded car. Peter Zahorecz apparently had various uniforms – boy scout, surgeon, mermaid, etc. – which he intended to wear for Neoast purposes. In the late afternoon we left the apartment and walked towards the Stockwell Gallery. On the street I kept my hand touching tENT's or Peter's shoulders. By chance we met Ottelie, Gordon W. and Theresa. My memory of these events is extremely unclear. They may (also) have happened the day before.

It may have been on this day that I spent several hours with Stiletto and visited his studio at PSI, a prestigious state-funded art centre. We entered the PSI Gallery and I shot footage of the artwork and was recorded commenting on it, as I was led by Stiletto through disorienting installations, before a bewildered curator. The commentary was primarily 'art historical'. The exhibition was based around the theme of the Korean demilitarised zone. I continued to film as we climbed up into the artist's studios, where no guests are allowed. Stiletto had been rebuked by the administration for not producing enough work to justify his studio, and so planned an occupation of Neoasts to compound their complaints. He left me alone in his barren room for an hour while he went to find a broken record player to burn with a blowtorch in a performance. As I waited blindly in the room, singing, whistling and clapping against its reverberation, I didn't realise that there was a pile of unravelled bared razor-wire on the floor in front of me.

Stiletto wanted to transport an object he had made across town from the PSI to his apartment. The object was a circular mirror called *Look Sharp,* the frame for which was a band of razor-wire. We carried it jointly, and without a case, onto the subway at rush hour, the train was packed and there was barely room to breathe. As we descended into the station, I hallucinated train lines like vast tentacles projecting from a coloured field located in my head. I felt extremely euphoric. On the train someone very nervously asked Stiletto what the razor-wire was, and he replied 'steel'.

We arrived at the Stockwell where a scene similar to the night before was taking place. Almost immediately someone I hadn't met dragged me across the room to where an 'installation' was and stuck my hand into broken glass and some thick goo, probably paint and glue mixed, which smeared all over me. Stiletto walked around with a lit blowtorch sticking out of his shoulder-bag. An evening of presentations was planned, with almost continual accompaniment from a boombox. I talked and messed around with people, a bunch of whom flipped me upside-down and made me run on my hands, out the door of the gallery and onto the street – and may have done the same to Theresa, I can't remember. Theresa made me run down the street at top speed, and made me bang my head on a stop sign.

At some point early on, we went to the Bridge Bookshop where tENT and I sold (or traded) a bunch of Widemouth tapes, and tENT was invited to work and run the store alone for an hour despite the fact that they had never met him before. He accepted and I had a charming conversation with Mami, whose shift he was supplementing, and then went for a cup of coffee with Debbie, before returning to the gallery. I found talking extremely difficult, although in many ways my entire experience suggested to me that socialising is more pleasurable without vision (at least under such circumstances).

During an action by Pamela Stockwell and friends, the cops arrived with threats of closing things down and met with verbal abuse and pacification. Theresa Rodrigues and I quickly cut eggplant on a table while the hatred grew. The police intervention reverberated for the rest of the evening, giving an excuse for fighting and dislike between the participants. A group of scrap-metal players dragged hundreds of pounds of metal into the gallery and engaged in playing, and then in altercations with Pamela Stockwell and one of the Karen Eliots. Both 'sides' tried to rally active support by forcing almost everyone in the space to talk about the conflict all night, thus preventing anything else from happening.

Peter and tENT tried to produce Booed Usic but were drowned out and ignored. Texts on the wall proclaiming the value of censorship, which had been crossed out, were duly followed by many of the participants. Steve threw a willing tENTATIVELY across the room like a beach-ball, after asking his permission, in an attempt to catalyse some slam dancing. Gordon W. prepared another meal for the participants and I played his Kohl Drum, after which he dedicated a short piece of drumming to me. As we left the gallery, one of the scrap-metal players stood outside screaming 'gentrifying bitch' at Pamela Stockwell.

We arrived at Stiletto's Neoast Hospital by ambulance. It was a temporary military installation occupying part of PSI, surrounded by bands of razor-wire preventing the entry of prying FDA inspectors. Inside the 'hospital', the Neoasts were to be cured of Neoasm in a sterile and featureless environment. Afterwards, the hospital would dissolve itself, as PSI regulations still required that no guests stay overnight, and no temporary Neoast health-care facilities be set up. We spent the night undergoing disorienting and painful treatment (including smooching), and in the end I was cured, at least temporarily, of Neoasm.

I spent the next day, *End of the World Saturday*, with Jamaica and Debbie, recovering, resting and playing, while tENTATIVELY and Peter left to participate in the *Flaming Iron March* in Tompkins Square Park, and the later festivities with Jack Smith, Gordon, Karen and some *Village Voice* reporters including Cindy Carr. The next day, which was the last day of the festival, everyone in the Unknown Neoast's apartment slept to make up for the disintegration of their sleep cycles. Norman, one of the Fourteen Secret Masters of the World, called from Baltimore with elliptical instructions to help Debbie free her car.

We put a lot of effort into cleaning the apartment to erase all traces of our illegal occupation; washing towels, drying out toilet paper, erasing messages on the answerphone and fabricating our own 'more believable ones', removing our smells. Somehow, we left the apartment with a surprise carride from Petty Quarl and went to Ricky Killreagan's pad, where the others deposited their belongings. We crossed the Lower East Side looking for a place to eat and finally realised we were way off schedule; we had missed the Williamsburg Bridge actions, the end of the festival. Happy but despondent, again cured of Neoasm, I was led to the Aztec Black-Light Bar. There the blindfold was removed, inducing several hours of schizophrenia and agonising confusion.

Slightly abridged from an illustrated pamphlet published by Dialectical Immaterialism Press in 1989, a few weeks after the events described took place.

WESSEX EXPOSED!

Equi-Phallic Alliance

This bulletin is produced as a response to the projection of place upon placelessness, to the fabrication of a 'Southern regional poetic', to cultural fascism in general and the imposition of destructive and picturesque aesthetics, a false cultural particularism, onto landscape, *poetic* and imagined (post-national) community in particular.

Dr Mintern, before his apparent death, had been working on what he referred to as 'a new poetry'. It seems clear that this poetic was formed beneath the false places we have found, being open to all poets and being placeless. This bulletin contains extracts from Dr Mintern's notes and fragments of reports received at HQ from our operatives in the underchalk as well as extracts from placeist documents.

> To any poet who is 'happening' (i.e. experiencing their own becoming) – rather than hoping to happen – place, politics, etc., are unavoidably transformed. In the sense that the placeists refer to place, place becomes irrelevant – territory is place in the process of being lost. You can't really own 'your' ground. A poetic that is entrapped within myth to the extent that it conceals its own synthetic nature, its inauthenticity, is one that has no real function outside of the mythical (virtual) world of the poets who use it. (To have a real function it must have meaning within the social realm, that is – it must include both its own, and the wider socio-cultural, inauthenticities.)
>
> All poetics are contained, but some are more tightly contained than others. A contained poetic, until it begins to

explore its own enclosure, remains socially useless. In that it confirms and replicates the processes of enclosure, within myth or ideology, it is socially harmful. It creates containment, it builds apparent distances as it unbuilds the means of crossing actual distances. It then becomes anti-poetic. Socially meaningless poetry is doubly displaced and may create double displacements in other people (these displacements are, I believe, responsible for both the psychic autotypes, or ghosts, and the physical replicants, accordingly). It constructs replicant people, replicant places and sentimental (often ideal-rural) cultures in place of the processes of being.

We believe that the death of Dr Mintern, as reported, is false and that a replicated Dr Mintern was murdered on the false landform called 'Wessex'. We believe him to have discovered actual place underneath 'place on stilts'.

A poetic that doesn't take and transform experience is one embedded in a myth of itself. A poetic that does take and transform experience may well, in demystifying it, prove the actuality of it to be other than originally perceived (i.e. poetry should help you to explode your paranoias, not confirm them).

The retrenchment implied in the whole approach of the Wessexist vanguard (rearguard might be a better term) suggests to us that their bundle of poetics holds the common feature of reinforcing the self-mything principle, thus leaving any hope of realisation within their poetries a vain one.

POETRY AND PLACELESSNESS

The Wessexists, as a group, seem to be caught up in a gathering dynamic based on deep-seated frustrations that 'the world' has failed to recognise the images they hold of themselves. There is a pronounced tendency amongst these increasingly fictional characters for them to attempt to 'live out' an idealised version of a 'poet's' life. Living such myths is, we think, self-destructive. Their poetry confirms their paranoia, which must be alarming.

Within their texts they put a great deal of effort into making out that their picturesque places are, in some way, both real and blessed by destiny.

The poetry of the south and southwest sometimes seems to be synonymous with 'the poetry of place' (although this too is an illusion). The 'Blandford elite' (Ha Ha) have attempted to possess and enclose this 'poetic ground' in order to exploit it, but – as such – they have become entrapped within their (mystified) experience of place. Thus they are unable to realise displacement (as process or otherwise). Place has become lost around their mythical corner, contained by their own mything of themselves.

'Poetry of place' has, traditionally, been a very conservative poetic (essentially pastoral). Jeremy Hooker seems conservative in his writing, but he actually emphasises (enacts) the displacements within Englishness, rather than reinforces them, so – as such – his working of that conservative poetic – a.k.a. 'ground' – is very (socially) useful (unlike the placeist thugs, he is able to realise the cultural actuality of placelessness). In his *Soliloquies*, Hooker does touch England's (cultural) ground, for real (it was a ground-breaking book). He is still involved in a process that began with these soliloquies (a process clearly concerned with the myth of the self). He explores the results of some of the processes of displacement from the very core of that displacement, from within the conservative poetic that has been the poetry of place. We don't think he has lost his edge; in fact we'd say he's on his way to new edges. That there is no room for us inside that tradition just means that we have to further transform (explode) it for ourselves (which is what any poet should be doing anyway). We can find our own new edges (and then expose them for the myths they are). Hopefully, within the process, we can find Dr Mintern.

Hooker's work provides us with a partial and virtual experience of a place none of us has ever seen, England. As for the great men of the south, they seem determined to reinforce the already emphatic conservative tendencies within that poetic (whilst at the same time supporting shoddy work, as if it were ground-breaking), without taking on the secondary gains they offer, whilst at the same time mystifying the poetic as a whole. In that a poem must be *made* it appears obvious that confirming and mystifying a process of containment within (and as) poetic (as picturesque) involves no creative activity at all. Hooker's work, on the other hand, provides us with both a window on England and a window on the processes that have displaced England (and on Hooker as an 'English' man). As progressives, what more could we ask of any poet? He has given us a glimpse of a (partial) map that contradicts both the map projected by the metropole and that presented by the petty regionalists.

SPREAD THE WORD, BEFORE THE WORD SPREADS YOU!

The Wessexist representation of their politics as radical is in one sense misguided (and absurd) and in another potentially dangerous. John Howard Darre, who recently joined the *Fears of the French* team, made some remarkable political statements in his *Vigilante* mag:

> England starves for brave leadership . . . If we do not vision our own choices . . . on this brave and beautiful island we shall fall voiceless into the nightmare . . . Our own political leeches, feeding off the creative blood of our people, will sell our national rights without shame . . . [We] need to rise up to assert our human rights in full national pride in our cultural heritage. Vigilante publications is to pursue a far more overtly political purpose. Our poetry interest will merge with *Fears of the French* where I shall take up the role of managing editor. The future is in the light and joy of independent communities freed of the sickness of centralised control.
>
> (Quotes from *Vigilant 9*, 'Open Press' supplement.)

This is a typically picturesque (Wessex) version of the 'blood and soil' national chauvinism that contributed so much to Hitler's fascism. That kind of emphasis on (your own) community and an implied corruption in anything universalist is typical of the pre-war Nazi broadsides against the Weimar republic (JHD does not seem too keen on closer ties with Europe.) The alternative is 'independent communities' (i.e. a regional centralisation that does not fragment the dead metropolitan centre, but replicates it in each so-called region, thus making the situation worse, not better: the ludicrous poetry of the Wessexists themselves illustrates the pompous guff such a sociocultural formation must produce; they really are their own worst enemies). Their aggregate position amounts to nothing more than an English Völkischism *(Length through Joy?)*. Hitler painted landscapes like the Wessexists write them.

These people are clearly enclosed within their own maddening myths (as are we all, if we become blinded or frustrated by ambition, humans being famously susceptible to conspiracy theories, rebirth myths and fables of easy heroism). Wessexists have become proto-fascist in both their world view and in their modus operandi (hysterical attacks on their 'enemies' being one of the more prominent social manifestations of this). In particular, they are increasingly fascist in a cultural sense, partly as an effect of the sociopolitical form their ambition is given or placed in (i.e. an imagined territory). They are pursuing their literary ambitions using imagined territory as a vehicle, replacing ultra-nationalism with ultra-regionalism. This is particularly the case with the Fatman and Mr Weedy. John Howard Darre seems to be caught *between* nation and region.

A PRECARIOUS ART

Dr Mintern has offered a number of scenarios that could be built into a new poetry of placelessness and, before his disappearance, he indicated that there might be many more such projections, as yet undisclosed (each one its own vagary). He seemed to think that there might be an infinite number of such poetries! If one aspect of our work in the Equi-Phallic Alliance is concerned with liberating 'nature' from the fascists (whatever 'nature' is when it's for real), then we couldn't do better than to start releasing mutant poetries now. That Dr Mintern believed that nature is synthetic is central to our strategy. We hope that by weakening containment within culture, our displaced poetries, mutating like they do, might weaken (and possibly explode) all other forms of containment. In the future, people could become real (it sounds absurd, we realise that, but we must try or be lost within the view). Places could deflate, replication and plagiarism end, even compression could fail and we could ignore the quest for self and place within processes of realisation (although this too could be myth). Dr Mintern is truly inauthentic. He appeared almost liberated before he left. The Wessex enclosers have enclosed nothing (*sic*) but myths of themselves!

Dr Mintern's excavations within the virtual Wessex proved, to him at least, that not only were all of the archaeological remains synthetically made, and placed, but that the chalk underneath the archaeology was also made, that it too is synthetic. If that is the case then all Wessex history is myth, right down to its version of the class struggle (that aspect in particular being cheesy in the extreme). He discovered the theory of the underchalk (and was the first person to postulate that caves are suspended in a wider void). Together with Barny, he proved that places are on stilts, that machineries exist that can raise and lower the elevation of place, as required, according to social conditions, in order to pacify the dispossessed, to quieten those who still suffer enclosure. Now we must finish his work.

A VARIOUS ENCLOSURE

One way to gauge the ideological content of a group is to study its social structure. If it is based on definition by expulsion, as the Wessexists are, we know to steer well clear. We also have a theory that elements in the Wessex group may themselves be trying to destroy Wessex by fatally infecting it with Situationism (that can only be to the good). It must be noted that the 'internationalism' of *Fears of the French* has more in common with the (virtual) internationalism of the Berlin

Olympic Games (universalist fascism being the post-war offering of its philosophers, it does fall into place (*sic*) rather (un)comfortably).

As it happens, the connections between 'England reborn' and Wessex do go back a long way. Wright's *Village that Died . . .* shows that up. Some very prominent English fascists have come from, or moved to, Dorset. Indeed, we have already received threatening and abusive letters from people who claim to be associated with *Southist* magazine. (It's unlikely that they are, but the claim could indicate their intentions, and the latest Wessex Projection does seem to be a nasty one.) Those letters came in envelopes festooned with English National Party stickers. One had 'For England and Wessex' written in biro across the top of the envelope.

These groups are, as yet, fragmented. (When mystified, the displacement process more effectively contains those who use it than its intended victims; fragmentation – on a sociopolitical level – is thus unavoidable.) What we have to do is to explode 'their' mystified (fictionalised) ground from underneath them before they can unite. If we achieve that they will be trapped within the mythical realm for ever. They will be of denied ideology (as entrapped as a Situationist). Once they are thus transfixed we can work them into narratives that unbuild distances and make (non-family-centred) communities (and thus places) real. It should be fairly straightforward.

LYRICAL ABSURDITIES

As far as conflicts between ourselves and other groups go, our position is mutually inclusive with that of the (very) exploded realist position (in the sense that what is called 'realism' is both self-consciously socially engaged and absurd) even though I do not believe that realism is any more real than symbolism (for instance).

Most 'new poetry' poets would agree that realism is essentially mythical, we think, and any who didn't would be daft, really. Strangely, one of the conceits of the new 'Wessex' fantasists is that what they say is, according to them, real. Our position privately is the same as that in our policy document (which you will all have received by now), that we are of an affinity with all inclusive poets, that we respect egalitarian inclusivity but that we must, within ideology, explode all exclusive hierarchies, and their myths and their mythical constructs (which include their places – in this case, Wessex).

It is ironic that by the very nature (*sic*) of the enclosing process, those who enclose themselves destroy themselves. That was shown up in the Fatman's review of the last Hooker book in *Fears of the French* (which was an attempt to enclose, or add value to, the work of Mr Weedy). The Fatman has been promoting Hooker as the (unwitting) grandfather of 'the South Movement' for years. It's typical that he should (a) turn against Hooker for ignoring the 'Southist' imperative and (b) use the review, in Weedy's mag, to promote Weedy as being a better poet than Hooker. The latter point is quite absurd – but Weedy is vain and *FOTF* is his mag. In that review the Fatman quoted from Weedy as much as he did Hooker. The review was a vehicle for Weedy's ego, with the Fat one licking his arse so deeply that his turdy tongue must have protruded from the Weedy mouth, making him into a fabulous beast, if not into an actual poet.

PANIC IN WESSEX

Poetic cleansing can seem to be an inadvertent and acceptable side-effect of (supposed) genius, at least some of the time. These superb poets are only following orders! At least that can be the Fatman's excuse, as that is exactly what he does (though he does have his own sneaky agenda): 'One benefit of their attempting to unite their individual visions of Wessex, a benefit of their attempting to unify, is that as their group widens the tensions within it build.' The Fatman has always tried to divide and rule, but he is very inept at it. Remarkably, up until recently he was still phoning us to slag off Mr Weedy, who in print he would have us believe is a genius. Whatever the

Fatman feels, we think he'll carry on mything out the same viewpoint until it consumes him. He seems to hope that if the coup attempt fails he can bail out of 'Wessex' and land back 'in' the social realm, but Wessex and his myths of that realm are indivisibly joined now; the former contains the latter. He has trapped himself in a dream world, well and truly. He was the one who set this thing in motion with his 'South Movement' (which at least dates back to 1987–88). If lightning is the symbol of the Wessex storm trooper, then we have seen lightning strike itself in the foot (Ha Ha). It serves them right.

The Wessexist rally in Huddersbland provided us with an ideal (*sic*) opportunity to see the proto-fascists at work within their enclosure. Their bundle (fasci) of poetics are becoming increasingly unstable. The mixture of territorial chauvinism, rebirth myth, the need they all seem to feel for domination and the myth they all seem to have that others have conspired against them to deprive them of their (natural) 'rights' forms an aggregate that has much in common with a (historically) fascist world view. That they are all, in their own ways, involved in enclosure – in denying rights and freedoms themselves within the prison of region, nation and/or meta-nation and poetic – seems to be becoming increasingly buried (mystified) under the myth that they have 'suffered' and that they are 'poor' (the latter claim in particular is not only absurd but also deeply offensive). The aggregate ideology is made up of myths perpetrated by individuals who have now combined, within their shared myth of what northern poets are about, to 'forge' a – more or less – shared position of what they suppose they 'need' to do to correct those 'wrongs'. In that 'forging' of their personal myths into one group myth they became proto-fascist.

MYTH AS METHOD

When the Fatman talks of 'the next palace revolution' (*FOTF* 12) being 'most likely instigated by the southwest' he is, typically, giving the game away. He certainly isn't talking about a 'caring socialism', he seems rather interested in kicking out (what he sees as) a totally corrupt regime and replacing it with another, with himself and Weedy as the bosses (Ha Ha). When he states that 'Armitage should . . . "escape the massacre"' (ibid.) he reveals his delusions of grandeur at their darkest (and his lack of irony). References to 'the killing jar' (FOTF 14) may be sinister or they may be an outward projection of this would-be poet's overpowering social death wish. There is certainly a self-fulfilling prophecy at work here, in which the myths created about poetry in the north will come true, but in the south and southwest (though, without the poems to back it up, this particular renaissance seems unlikely to exist outside of myth). Self-fulfilling prophecy has a tendency towards its own irony, despite the narrator. Myths consume themselves. If the landscapes collapse, as Dr Mintern predicted they will, all EPA agents should be sure to be outside the myth zone, or we could lose you to the narrative. If that point arrives we will really have to get real. If they don't bring the landscape down with their (unrealised) absurdisms, we'll do it ourselves with our realised ones!

The Fatman has already started to crow about a 'huge pot of money' he and Weedy have allegedly been 'promised'. He told us about it in the same rant about Blandford being imminently reborn as 'the New Huddersfield', with its tower blocks all thatched and with 're-educated' northerners in Wessex costume, all happily singing regional songs and bowing cheerily to giant chalk-cut portraits of Weedy and the Fat one (each totalitarian hill will be hallmarked, apparently). The meadows south of Blandford did shimmer slightly at sunset, on the appointed day, but Huddersfield remained firmly fixed in the north. Further, their obnoxious publications have done no harm at all to poets in the north but have caused varieties of harm to those who work in what was the south of England (the assault on the north has been laughable). It's bizarre, the way in which those possessed by Utopia will try to destroy useful actualities in order to attempt to build something that is unbuildable, in order to place the placeless (we are up against nerds).

RIDICULOUS LANDSCAPES

These people know very little about landscapes and even less about the forces that make and possess them. It seems daft that they can't work out that the 'northern scene' is a focus of the (post-)national scene and is not, as such, 'regional' (it would be really crap if it were). This wider scene is one from which the Southist brethren are increasingly opting out, since their books have received few good reviews – and those written by each other. I think any poet who is going to 'make it' has to transform what is around them anyway (rather than transcend it into myth); all scenes are a containment (and an illusion). No happening poet can be so contained (so what Southists see as the cause of their failure is in fact irrelevant to it). If we can't transform the scene we perceive then we are just not a poet. Any poet who does transform their scene will get respect anywhere, no matter where they live or where the foci of the (post-)national poetry scene happens to be. Those who don't offer such respect are fools (which neatly brings us back to Wessex, the South, our Shining Territories of the Southwest, wherever).

> The current threat to actual (cultural) transformation comes from those proto-fascist tendencies which unfortunately exist within the cultural currents that make up the poetry scene overall, but which are socially material (apparent) in the actions of a small group of poets more or less local to ourselves. In exploding place we also explode the myth of Wessex. Doubt everything.

We believe that Dr Mintern is still alive and in the underchalk. He would not indulge in martyrdom (leave that to the placeists). We will get him back before we bring the landscape down and effect the realisation of social injustice (and thus of justice).

FORWARD WITH THE MISSION OF THE EPA! DESTROY THE VIEW
UPON WHICH THE LAW IS BUILT! EXPLODE THE FOUNDATIONS
OF THE STATE! LET THERE BE NO LANDSCAPE TO OWN! EVERY-
WHERE IS NOWHERE! REALISATION NOW! UNITY IS LENGTH!

*Odu verlorener Gott! Du unend liche Spur! Nur weil dich
reifsend zuletzt die Feindschaft verteilte, sind wir die Hörenden
jetzt und ein Mund der Natur.*

First published in *The Listening Voice: Newsletter of the Equi-Phallic Alliance
(Induction Bulletin – Men's Section)* 1, Summer 1996.

CHEW ON THIS

Chewing gum and the rise of Glop Art

Luther Blissett

Following hard on the heels of the media hype surrounding Damien Hirst comes an underground backlash in the form of Glop Art. Owing a debt to the graffiti movement of the eighties, Glop Artists modify advertising posters with the aid of chewing gum. The most common forms of Glop Art are indecent sculptures, with the gum placed so that it protrudes from human orifices. Every Glop Artist has their own obsession. One is said to specialise in hanging fake snot from the nostrils of the pop singer Sting.

Rather than adopting the amoral stance of the current crop of gallery darlings, whose activity serves to turn art into a commodity, Glop Artists turn a commodity (chewing gum) into art. As such, Glop Art represents the cutting edge of critical thinking among outsider artists whose opposition to all forms of capitalist culture manifests itself as a self-conscious ethical positioning. Glop Art straddles the divide between culture and petty crime, although whether practitioners should be charged with littering or vandalism seems to be a moot point among legal experts. Fear of being dragged through the courts makes Glop Artists elusive; they can't be contacted through the normal art-world channels and they don't have press agents. However, manic gum-chewing combined with staggering and slurred speech are the tell-tale characteristics of the Glopper. Please note, it isn't always safe to approach Glop

Artists when they are in the tired and emotional state that frequently accompanies their illicit activities.

I encountered an anonymous practitioner on the escalators of Leicester Square tube station and asked him how he got started. 'I was coming home from a club and I wanted to get rid of my gum but there were no bins because they'd been removed after an IRA bomb. So I just stuck the gum on a poster, over a model's face. I thought it looked quite funny. After that I found myself in similar situations, and I started being more creative about it.'

A spokesman for London Transport Authority Advertising refused to comment on the Glop movement, although he did say that posters are changed when defaced but having to do this is an inconvenience. My Leicester Square contact didn't have much sympathy for the advertising industry. 'I don't like the way the media makes people feel inadequate. Faces are the best targets to attack because the models are always so ridiculously perfect that they look inhuman, so it brings them down to earth.' However, this particular Glop artist was dismissive of the increasingly common practice of adding genitalia to models of both sexes. He hadn't heard of Hannah Wilke, the America feminist who makes chewing gum sculpture in vulva shapes.

Despite my new friend's scanty knowledge of art history, it was obvious to me that his activities formed part of a hoary cultural tradition. Both his work and that of the Glasgow Glop artist who specialises in adding extra limbs to the models featured on street posters brought to mind the activities of François Dufrêne and Jacques de la Villeglé. In the late fifties, these two Nouveau Realistes exhibited layered street hoardings that they'd carefully ripped and torn. Then there was Wolf Vostell, a key member of the Fluxus group, who in the sixties produced a magazine entitled *De-coll/age*. Likewise, in one of his thirty-five-year-old auto-destructive art manifestos, Gustav Metzger proclaimed that: 'In the evenings some of the finest works of art produced now are dumped on the streets of

Soho ... Auto-destructive art is an attack on capitalist values and the drive to nuclear annihilation.'

Auto-destructive art works were made by flinging acid onto canvases and similar techniques. According to Metzger: 'Auto-destructive paintings, sculptures and constructions have a life time varying from a few moments to twenty years.' Glop Art fits neatly into this framework, since an army of street cleaners regularly remove it from hoardings all over the country. Nevertheless, a cleaner I found washing floors at Leicester Square tube station did not see himself as part of the movement: 'It's a dirty business having to remove haloes from above Pamela Anderson's head,' he informed me. 'Dealing with chewing gum is one of the hardest parts of this job.'

Prior to my Leicester Square field trip, I'd canvassed numerous experts for their opinions and had been unable to find a single British critic who'd rise to the challenge of giving Glop Art serious attention. Eventually I obtained the home number of Patric O'Brien, who'd been affiliated to the Scandinavian Institute for Comparative Vandalism, an organisation set up by the Danish painter Asger Jorn. At one point in his career, Jorn produced a series of what he called modified paintings, which were bad works he'd bought cheaply in flea markets and then partially painted over with delightful abstract swirls.

O'Brien was very excited when I phoned him. He promised to come to Britain later this summer so that he could scrutinise Glop Art at close quarters. He also urged me to seek out the study of the graffiti in Normandy churches that Jorn had produced in association with such luminaries as the archaeologist P.V. Glob, author of *The Bog People*. 'I don't doubt that a proper evaluation of Glop Art will cause critics to question the received structure of art history,' O'Brien told me. 'That was what Jorn intended when he began his investigations into medieval graffiti. Glop Art is the purest manifestation of the human need to create and manipulate images, therefore it should be a part of art history. It will transform the discipline by shattering the elitist framework adopted by the majority of contemporary critics.'

I put some of this to the clubber I met at Leicester Square. 'What a load of cobblers,' he laughed before heading for the Northern Line. I shuffled my feet and looked at the ground. Then I was struck by a flash of inspiration. The gum on the floor of the Tube station was suddenly far more interesting than any consciously made intervention intended to subvert the manufactured environment that surrounded me. This casually discarded gum had blackened and was thickly layered, bringing to mind the work of Malevich. The latest advances in Glop Art are the product of thousands of shuffling feet. The best kinds of folk art have always been completely anonymous. O'Brien was right: 'To bring Glop Art into mainstream critical discourse will perhaps create confusion. The risk is enormous but it has to be taken, this is an opportunity for cultural renewal.'

First published in *The Big Issue* 183, 27 May 1996.

CONTACTS

Although opposition to 'consensus reality' is as old as recorded history, groups organising against it tend to be transitory. By the time you read this, it's likely that at least some of the people listed will have moved on. Don't be dispirited if your mail is returned unopened, just try another address. Some groups last only weeks or months, others are active for years. The London Psychogeographical Association was set up in 1992 with the intention that it would be dissolved in 1997. I've included the LPA in this listing, but unless you write to them within six months of this book being published, you're unlikely to receive a reply. This isn't a definitive list of contacts, it's just a bunch of addresses that will be useful to anyone interested in the material anthologised in the preceding pages.

Association of Autonomous Astronauts. Unlike bureaucratic state-controlled space agencies, the AAA develops as a non-hierarchical network of like-minded groups around the world dedicated to local community-based space-exploration programmes. For a full list of AAA groups please write to one of the addresses below.

AAA Rosko, c/o Ewen Chardronnet, 59 Rue Lepic, 75018 Paris, France.
Publishes *Gravité Zéro* newsletter. Send French stamps or international reply coupons for copies.

AAAUX, 64 Beechgrove, Aberhonddu, Powys, Wales LD3 9ET. e-mail: AAA@fnord.demon.co.uk

AAA-Paris Sud, c/o C. Cauchy, 92 rue Didot, 75014 Paris, France.

Inner City AAA, BM Jed, London WC1N 3XX, UK. e-mail: AAA@pHreak.Intermedia.co.uk. Web site: http://www.deepdisc.com/AAA
Publishes *Escape From Gravity* newsletter. Send British stamps or international reply coupons for copies.

Radio AAA, BM Box 3641, London WC1N 3XX, UK. e-mail: AAA@uncarved.demon.co.uk
Publishes *Ad Astra!* newsletter. Send British stamps or international reply coupons for copies.

Associazione Psicogeografica di Isernia, c/o G. Venditti, via Gorizia 1, 86170 Isernia, Italy.

Associazione Psicogeografica di Milano, c/o M. Montanari, via Marco D'Oggiono 12, 20123 Milano, Italy.

autonome a.f.r.i.k.a.-gruppe, c/o Edition Nautilus, Am Brink 10, 21029 Hamburg, Germany.
Rigorously anonymous collective interested in developing the theory and practice of the communication guerrilla; for this reason they have reviewed actions by other groups such as the Tübingen-based Committee for Public Safety and Luther Blissett Network.

Nigel Ayers, see under *Network News*.

Mandy B., c/o BM Jed, London WC1N 3XX, UK.
Pissing all over every received idea about decorum and good taste. Go with the flow!

Break/Flow, 89 Vernon Road, Stratford, London E15 4DQ, UK.
Magazine featuring Ronald Sukenick, Schizopolitics for Scallies, Alexander Trocchi, Debord, Wolman, TransEuro Underground, TechNET, Praxis, Reviews, Dissing, and Careering. £2 per issue, published irregularly.

Bureau of Unitary Cosmopolitanism, c/o Patrick Mullins, PO Box 203, Portland, OR 97207, USA.
Neither physics nor metaphysics!

By-Pass, PO Box 148, Hove, East Sussex BN3 3DQ, UK.
Caption reviews of 'underground' publications with addresses and ordering information.

College of Omphalopsychism, 48 College Road, Manchester M16 8FH, UK.
Enabling you to put your mind in your navel; take part in the Conspiracy of Equals; enter the inner library of Universal Knowledge; speak the long-lost Language of the Birds; achieve oneness with the Great Omphalos; and contemplate the Uncreated Light in the afterglow of a metastatic orgasm. Publishes the journal *Man In A Suitcase*. Send a British stamp or international reply coupon.

Corporate Art Project, 10 Francis Street, Brightlingsea, Essex CO7 0DG, UK.
Publishes irregular newsletter with features on subjects such as the strange alignments of various new towns. Currently involved in efforts to revive Outer Spaceways Incorporated, the legendary Essex psychogeographical outfit of the early seventies.

DADAnarchist Art Foundation, c/o Thee Data Base, P.O. Box 1238, Glasgow, Scotland G12 8AB.
The DADAnarchists perform spontaneous acts of violence against the imagination (i.e. the reproduction of state ideology in the minds of individuals). They were responsible for *KII*, an experimental performance project, where they infamously locked over forty people in a freight container for the evening. Their latest project is the Society for the Termination of Art (START), who recently levitated the new Gallery of Modern Art in Glasgow. START's manifesto proclaims 'Culture is dead: all that remains now is to bury it.' The 'Termination of Art' ceremony will take place at the

Necropolis in Glasgow on Burns Night in the year 2003. For further information send a large SAE.

Decadent Action, BM Decadence, London WC1N 3XX, UK. Decadent Action is a London-based consumer-terrorist organisation, who have broken with the traditional thinking of left and anarchist groups in fully embracing the capitalist marketplace. Rather than ignoring and boycotting capitalism, Decadent Action plan to make it destroy itself through overspending and over-consumption. They employ the simple rules of demand and supply economics much as their less elegant counterparts would employ a molotov. They are most cherished for their attestation that they wish capitalism to die a rock 'n' roll death, fat and bloated, choking on its own vomit. A sample issue of their newsletter *The Decadent* can be obtained for an SAE or $1.

Dialectical Immaterialism, PO Box 22142, Baltimore, MD 21203, USA.
e-mail: johnb@berndtgroup.net. Web site: http://www.berndtgroup.net/berndt/reference
Superficial responses to a 'truthless' world' are a momentary stopgap to a new truth of some kind, a new integration of reality. New beliefs rush to fill the gap – a gap that, from a nihilistic standpoint, never existed. The fact that 'there is no truth' is taken to imply something. However mentally liberating this may seem, no implications can honestly be attributed to this revelation, and to the extent that it is completed, it should be utterly uninstructive, but not equal to what it discredits.

Equi-Phallic Alliance, 33 Hartington Road, Southampton, Hants SO14 0EW, UK.
Spread the word before the word spreads you! The Equi-Phallic Alliance has undertaken a programme of cultural extermination of all unrealised poetries. This essential work is a part of a wider decompression that we expect to conclude with the creation and destruction of Utopia by the year 2000.

This enactment of the palin-genetic myth is intended to illustrate the absurdity of all cultural formations founded on particularities of place, language or historical process. There is no poetic beyond the poetic of containment. Destroy all pomposities now. We have imagined placelessness and already places have ceased to exist. The landscape is falling! The hills are scenic and they sway on their stilts! Join us and help to destroy England! Unity is length! To further these aims, the EPA publish *The Listening Voice* and organise excursions into the underchalk.

Matthew Fuller, c/o BM Jed, London WC1N 3XX, UK.
Mad, bad and dangerous to know.

Gruppe M, c/o Horn, Bayerische Str. 30, 10707 Berlin, Germany.
Began in 1991 with unadvertised outdoor exhibitions, secrecy was the big thing and anonymity was fun. Subsequently concentrated on writing and readings, first book published in 1994. In 1996 it was revealed that Gruppe M consisted of Claudia Basrawi, Michael Horn and Mario Mentrup.

Kinokaze, c/o Mischievous Productions, PO Box 8868, London SE16 1ZF.
Magazine that reports from the 'underground' with the emphasis on cinema, drugs and performance art.

London Psychogeographical Association, Box 15, 138 Kingsland High Street, London E8 2NS, UK.
Conspiracy theories generally portray recent history as the product of secret processes that leave the reader feeling powerless and vulnerable in a world organised by strange cults. In this vulnerable state, the victim of conspiracy theory is then susceptible to recruitment by precisely the sort of cult that they have been induced to fear. In fact, the propagation of a conspiracy theory entails the organisation of a counter-conspiracy, so that in effect the meme of conspiracy is transferred to the oppositional tendency, and thus opposition is recuperated. Our modus operandi is completely opposed

to this. We are not unmasking a successful conspiracy, for example, the murder of JFK. Rather, we are exposing a conspiracy before it reaches its culmination. The essence of our approach is that we seek to prevent what we've predicted from happening. If our goal is achieved, and the ritual murder of Prince Charles does not take place, we will have substantially weakened the psychogeographical subjugation of the proletariat. Of course, all our theories will be dismissed out of hand as an asinine joke, but this is infinitely preferable to our fate should we fail to prevent our prediction from being realised.

Luther Blissett Project, c/o APB, Signor Guglielmi, CP 744, 40100 Bologna Centrale, Italy. e-mail: nav0243@iperbole.bologna.11
Man of the moment!

Luther Blissett Situationautic Theatre, c/o R Pacossi, via Fossoli 4, 41100 Modena, Italy.
Makes Artaud look like Andrew Lloyd Webber.

Manchester Area Psychogeographic, 24 Burlington Road, Withington, Manchester M20 4QA, UK.
MAP has been in circulation since December 1995. Its aim is to change the way the conurbation of Manchester is perceived and used, as a lived-in environment. To achieve that change, MAP detects the ancient reverberations of the buried city, and traces the alignments that have, throughout history, channelled and controlled the emotions of the city-dweller. Supporters and sympathisers are invited to take part in regular MAP actions, which began on February 1996 when we levitated the Manchester Corn Exchange, commemorating the 400th anniversary of the arrival in Manchester of Dr John Dee, astrologer, alchemist, cartographer, code maker, and Warden of Manchester's collegiate Church. We publish a free newsletter every two months – just send a stamp (first or second class) and your address.

Melancholic Troglodyte, Box MT, 121 Railton Road, Herne Hill, London SE24, UK.

Dual language English/Persian magazine. Look at the ceilings of your mosques, mullah-bourgeois – see how it carries more cracks than the face of an old, tired whore? Would it be sufficient, I wonder, for a melancholic troglodyte to roar out a primal scream to bury you under centuries of tradition and bigotry. Fear the Melancholic Troglodytes, fear the Hermaphrodite International!

Neoist Alliance, BM Senior, London WC1N 3XX, UK.

Our production of a discourse that is simultaneously artificial and natural began with the levitation of the Brighton Pavilion in May 1993. Our aim was to disrupt the normal temporality of a Stockhausen concert by following *and* anticipating tradition. This and other actions have brought about the dissolution of the restricted accord of the concept in the subjective quickening of our cognitive faculties. The Neoist Alliance newsletter *Re:Action* is issued 'irregularly' on the winter and summer solstices.

Network News, PO Box 2, Lostwithiel, Cornwall, PL22 0YY, UK.

e-mail: earthly@draught.demon.co.uk.

Sinister beasts, earth mysteries, the occult shenanigans of the royal family, the occult symbolism of British currency, time travelling punk rockers, Nocturnal Emissions merchandising and much, much more.

Photostatic, c/o Lloyd Dunn, 521 Church Street, Apt. 2, Iowa City, IA 52245–2003, USA.

Magazine focusing on copy culture, marginal arts, electronic music, critical commentary on the 'underground', etc.

Preliminary Committee for the Founding of a New Lettrist International, c/o London Psychogeographical Association, Luther Blissett Project or Neoist Alliance.

Shake in your shoes, bureaucrats! The international power of

the Druid Councils will soon wipe you out! Long live the
General Strike! Long live revolutionary communism!

The Spectaclist, 15091 Robin Street, San Leandro, CA
94578–1964, USA. e-mail: rfear@mills.edu.
A speculative journal of arts, media and culture. Aesthetics,
commodities and the body, towards a cultural poetics. Post-
Situationist, heavily involved with copy culture and issues
related to plagiarism and copyright.

Super! Bierfront, c/o HW, PO Box 335, 10925 Berlin,
Germany.
Satirical German language magazine. Recent articles include
'Is Michael Jackson a Poetic Terrorist??!!!' and 'Is Prince
Charles Hitler?' Essential reading.

Thee Temple Ov Psychick Youth.
Now defunct but some former members can be contacted
c/o RADIO AAA, BM Box 3641, London WC1N 3XX, UK.
e-mail: AAA@uncarved.demon.co.uk

The Wobbler, PO Box 5059, London W12 7ZT. e-mail:
ziontrain@onelove.demon.co.uk. Web site: http://
www.china.co.uk/china/ziontrain
Weird shit, conspiracy theories, dope, agit-prop, excellent dub
and Zion Train merchandise.